WHAT PEOPLE ARE SAYING ABOUT

Sing Out for Justice

This is an excellent, highly readable introduction to the Hebrew prophets, one which brings them to life and makes them speak to our own perceptions and concerns. The author has an all-too-rare knack of making honest biblical scholarship entertaining and relevant, and manages to clarify awkward issues of date, authorship and history without ever being boring. It should be strongly recommended to anyone who thinks the Old Testament is dull.

The Very Revd Dr Jeffrey John, Dean of St Albans

Ray Vincent is a master of his brief with a deep knowledge and understanding of the prophets. Not only will we want to look again at the original texts but he brings them to life and ignites our imagination making them relevant for us today. This is an exciting book that at times embraces us and carries us along at a speed that is worthy not only of a scholar but of an award winning novelist!

The Revd Lord Roger Roberts of Llandudno

This book will certainly appeal to preachers and pastors, and to others looking for resources for Bible Study in church life. But it will also be of value to those who are looking for inspiration to see the world differently, and to find strength and encouragement to challenge the unjust powers that dominate so much of modern life. From politics to peaceful living, the Hebrew Prophets call to the depths of the human condition and invite transformation and change. *Sing Out for Justice* brings their words to life once more.

Dr Simon Woodman, Co-Minister of I
Church, London; author of *The Book o*
2008)

T0162976

I am indebted to Ray Vincent for this timely contribution to the theological and public conversation on social justice. I have every confidence that his work will be valued and well received. I very much appreciate this valuable reflection.

The Revd Canon Aled Edwards, OBE, Chief Executive, Cytûn/Churches Together in Wales

Ray Vincent gives us the whole of the prophetic literature back as scripture, bringing each prophet's voice to life within a beautifully concise overview of their settings and situations. He enables each to speak anew by drawing parallels with challenges we face today. The result is a dynamic encounter with some of the most passionate religious insight ever put into writing.

The Revd Roberta Rominger, United Church of Christ Pastor, Former General Secretary of the United Reformed Church

The Old Testament prophets are little read and poorly understood, yet we need their teaching for the 21st century. Ray Vincent introduces them with a story-teller's eye and shares their heart for justice.

Dr Tim Bulkeley, Honorary Lecturer in Theology, University of Auckland

Sing Out for Justice

The Passion and Poetry of the Hebrew Prophets

Sing Out for Justice

The Passion and Poetry of the Hebrew Prophets

Ray Vincent

CHRISTIAN
ALTERNATIVE

Winchester, UK
Washington, USA

First published by Christian Alternative Books, 2017
Christian Alternative Books is an imprint of John Hunt Publishing Ltd.,
Laurel House, Station Approach,
Alresford, Hants, SO24 9JH, UK
office1@jhpbooks.net
www.johnhuntpublishing.com
www.christian-alternative.com

For distributor details and how to order please visit the 'Ordering' section on our website.

Text copyright: Ray Vincent 2016

ISBN: 978 1 78099 923 4
978 1 78099 927-2 (ebook)
Library of Congress Control Number: 2016961474

A CIP catalogue record for this book is available from the British Library.

Design: Stuart Davies

Printed and bound by CPI Group (UK) Ltd, Croydon, CR0 4YY, UK

We operate a distinctive and ethical publishing philosophy in all areas of our business, from our global network of authors to production and worldwide distribution.

CONTENTS

Preface

Like most people brought up in the Christian faith, I grew up with Bible stories. In the New Testament there were the stories of Jesus and the adventures of Peter and Paul. In the Old Testament there were the exciting tales of Noah and the Ark, Joseph and his coat of many colours, Moses and the crossing of the Red Sea, Samson, Gideon, David and Goliath, Elijah on Mount Carmel, and so many others. We also memorised one or two of the shorter Psalms like "The Lord is my shepherd", or "I will lift up mine eyes unto the hills". But the books of the prophets – all those books from Isaiah to Malachi – were largely an unknown country. When I grew older I felt it was my duty to try to read them, but usually couldn't make much sense of them. Their language was obscure, solemn, forbidding and full of strange names. This is still the experience of most people today, even those who conscientiously try to read the Bible regularly.

There are two main reasons for this. One is that these books are rather short on good stories. A few exceptions stand out, such as Jonah and the whale, Daniel in the den of lions, and the three men in the fiery furnace. Apart from these bits almost the only passages in the prophets that are at all familiar are those that feature in Handel's Messiah and Christmas carol services.

Another reason why Christians tend not to read this part of the Bible is that they have been taught to read the Bible through the eyes of the central Christian beliefs, and this often makes it difficult to appreciate the prophets. There is a feeling that they are either inconsistent with Christian beliefs or irrelevant, seeming not to say much about them. The story on which traditional Catholic and Protestant Christianity is based may be summed up in a few sentences. God created human beings to be in fellowship with him, but the disobedience of Adam and Eve broke that relationship and condemned all future generations to sin and death. God sent his Son Jesus Christ into the world to make atonement by bearing our sins on the cross and to rise again to give us eternal life. Because of this, those who put their faith in Jesus have their sins forgiven and will go to heaven when they die, but those who reject him will go to hell. Of course there are variations in the way this message is understood. Catholics and Protestants have a slightly different slant on it, and there are "liberal" interpretations that question some of the details, but the essential pattern has remained much the same for centuries.

The Bible material on which this pattern of belief is founded is mostly in the opening chapters of Genesis, the New Testament accounts of the life, death and resurrection of Jesus, and the epistles of Paul. It is difficult to see what the prophets add to it. There are individual passages that are quoted as prophecies of Christ, but the prophets for the most part seem to have very little to say about this message of personal sin, atonement and eternal life.

On the other hand, many of us today are inspired by another theme in the Bible. We look at the tragic state of the world with its poverty, injustice, war and oppression, and the good news we look for is justice and peace. We see "salvation" as the world being saved from the self-destruction to which it seems to be heading. We find inspiration in the stories of God siding with the underdog and setting people free. The centre of it all is Jesus: his radical message of universal love, his crucifixion in which we see reflected all the victims of the injustice and cruelty of the world, and the message of resurrection in which we sense that life overcomes death, love overcomes hate and good overcomes evil.

Many of the world's conflicts today seem to be bound up with religion, and we feel that if the world needs a faith at all it must be one that expresses the universal hopes and visions of humanity rather than a collection of doctrines that divide us from one another. It must also be a faith that offers a hope of *this* world being changed rather than just the comforting assurance that if we are good, or if we have the right beliefs, we will go to heaven when we die.

If we turn to the prophets with this kind of quest they come leaping to life, because that is the very thing they were talking about most of the time. The anger that has put many people off reading them was not the grim, puritanical "righteousness" we associate with pious old-fashioned preachers. It was raw and contemporary. It was the kind of anger we see in present-day demonstrators, marchers and protest singers. They had a passion for justice and saw disaster looming unless the nation changed its ways. At the same time they had exciting visions of a different world, a world of peace and plenty enjoyed not by the few but by everyone.

The prophets were poets. It is not enough to say that they teach us to practise justice. They do not "teach" in that kind of way. They long for justice, they lament the lack of justice, they keep alive the hope for justice, and they celebrate justice. An important part of their message is that the world is not changed simply by denunciation or argument, though there is plenty of both in the prophets. It needs songs and dreams.

I hope this book will encourage people to read the prophets and draw inspiration from them for their quest for justice in today's world. It needs a little imagination, and for some of us a new approach, to do this. So often we have been taught to read the Bible rather solemnly, asking, "What is God saying to me here about my personal spiritual life?" I am convinced that we will get much more out of it if we approach it with an open mind and more down-to-earth questions. Why did anybody bother to say this? And after it was said, why did anybody take the trouble to write it down? What kind of person would say this? What kind of mood were they in? Were they angry, bitter, frightened, questioning, defiant, tender, joyful, playful, lyrical? What kind of situation made them say what they said? What were they speaking *against*? Can we imagine someone disagreeing with them, and if so what was that person saying? And why was the issue so important? It is when we ask questions like this that we begin to feel the passions that moved the prophets to speak and to see how relevant they are to our own time.

I would like to acknowledge with thanks the help and encouragement I have received from Tim Bulkeley, Peter and Barbara Clark, Aled Edwards, John Henson, Jeffrey John, Vaughan Rees, Roger Roberts, Roberta Rominger, Stanley and Diana Soffa, Janet Tollington, Peter and Mary West, Simon Woodman and a number of other friends, some of whom prefer to remain anonymous. I have also benefited from the observations of friends in the Progressive Christianity Network and other discussion groups, and people who have spurred me on by constantly asking when my next book was coming out!

This book is a kind of introduction to the prophets, but not a textbook. To quote a recent writer on a different but related topic:

"This is not a scholarly book but it is an enthusiastic one and I just hope that some of its enthusiasm will catch." (Mark Oakley, *The Splash of Words: Believing in Poetry*, Canterbury Press 2016, p xvi).

A word about terminology: the specific name of the God of Israel is denoted in Hebrew by the letters YHWH. Hebrew was originally written with consonants only, so we cannot be certain of how it was pronounced. The general agreement of scholars is that it was something like "Yahweh". However, it came to be regarded as too holy to be uttered by human lips, and it became customary when reading aloud to replace it with "the Lord". When vowels were introduced into the biblical text the name was given the vowels of "the Lord" in order to remind the reader what to say. In Latin the Hebrew consonants became JHVH, and English Bibles, following the Latin, wrote it as it appeared in the Hebrew text, resulting in the name "Jehovah", with the consonants of one word and the vowels of another! In most English Bibles it is rendered as "the LORD" (in block capitals). Where the title "Lord" occurs together with the name, it is usually rendered as "the Lord GOD". In this book we observe this usage.

Biblical quotations, except where otherwise stated, are from the Good News Bible.

1

The Street Preacher

It was festival time in the hill town of Bethel. The fragrance of incense mingling with the smell of roasting beef and goat drifted out from the temple, where offerings were being made to the great golden bull that represented the God of Israel. The space by the town gate – the place where people usually gathered to transact business and share the latest gossip – was heaving with people and carts. Families were coming in from the countryside with their offerings of fruit and grain and their animals to be slaughtered. Those who had already made their offering were on the way out to find a space where the family could sit down together and eat the meat. Traders were selling their wares, entertainers were gathering an audience. The beggars were busier than ever, knowing by experience that people feel a bit more generous at festival time.

In one corner there was a little gathering around a stranger who seemed to be preaching. This too was a common feature of feast days. Some were listening to this preacher avidly, some were cheering, whilst others were murmuring their disagreement or walking away in disgust. Snatches of the preacher's words could be heard above the hubbub in the square.

"The LORD says, I hate your religious festivals; I cannot stand them! When you bring me burnt-offerings and grain-offerings, I will not accept them... Stop your noisy songs; I do not want to listen to your harps...

Who was this? Some kind of anti-religious fanatic? But he seemed to be speaking in the name of God! What kind of blasphemy was this? He was even making God sound sarcastic:

"The Sovereign LORD says, People of Israel, go to the holy place in Bethel and sin, if you must!... Go ahead and offer your bread in thanksgiving to God, and boast about the extra offerings you bring! This is the kind of thing you love to do."

What right had this intruder, probably a foreigner, to come and attack the holy place? Bethel was an ancient shrine, built on the spot where Jacob, the ancestor of the whole nation, had dreamed of a ladder stretched between earth and heaven with angels going up and down on it. It was Jacob himself who had set up a stone pillar and named the place Beth-El, "house of God". What was this stranger ranting about?

Those who listened a bit more closely understood why the crowd around him were mostly the poorer people. He was attacking the rich traders who:

"... sell into slavery honest men who cannot pay their debts, poor men who cannot repay even the price of a pair of sandals. They trample down the weak and helpless and push the poor out of the way..."

He was talking about the women in the capital city calling to their husbands for more wine as they oppress and crush the poor – "fat cows", he called them! He described the rich lying on ivory beds, feasting on meat, singing idle songs, drinking wine by the bowlful and massaging themselves with the finest perfumes, oblivious to the plight of their neighbours and the desperate state of the nation.

"What desperate state?" people might well have asked. The kingdom of Israel at that time (around 760 BC) was enjoying a period of peace and prosperity. It was also a time when religious observance was very popular. People offered generous gifts to the priestly establishment, paid their tithes meticulously and flocked to the temples for the festivals. They believed the prosperity they were enjoying was a sign of God's blessing, a reassurance that they were a special, exceptional people.

But this preacher was determined to prick the bubble of their self-satisfaction. What made them so sure they were specially favoured? They believed that God had brought them out of

Egypt and given them this land. So what? Who brought the Ethiopians and the Philistines and the Arameans to the places they now inhabit? God's judgments are based not on favoured nations but on what is good and right. In any case, even if they are right in thinking they are the chosen people it might make things harder for them rather than easier:

"Of all the nations on earth, you are the only one I have known and cared for. That is what makes your sins so terrible, and that is why I must punish you for them."

The preacher was turning his satire on the people who, while they were worshipping, were secretly saying to themselves:

"We can hardly wait for the holy days to be over so that we can sell our corn. When will the Sabbath end, so that we can start selling again? Then we can overcharge, use false measures, and tamper with the scales to cheat our customers. We can sell worthless wheat at a high price…"

This kind of "worship", he was saying, was sickening to God. What God wants is not empty praise but people acting justly. He can do without rituals and hymns, but as for justice, he can never get enough of it. He longs for it like a desert land crying out for water:

"Let justice flow like a stream, and righteousness like a river that never goes dry."

The preacher was Amos. All these quotations are found in his book (Amos 5:21-23; 4:4-5; 2:6-7; 4:1; 6:4-6; 3:2; 8:5-6; 5:24). Amos came from the hill country of Tekoa in the kingdom of Judah, Israel's neighbour to the south. The two kingdoms were really one nation, worshipping the same God, but they had been separated because of a dispute after the death of King Solomon nearly two hundred years before.

Amos's preaching understandably drew the attention of the established powers in Israel. When he predicted that because of all the injustice and oppression going on in the kingdom King Jeroboam II would die a violent death, it was the last straw.

Amaziah, the priest in charge of the shrine at Bethel, sent a report to the king. Then he turned to Amos and told him to go back to his own country and "earn your bread there, and prophesy there." Amos's response was:

"I am no prophet, nor a prophet's son; but I am a herdsman, and a dresser of sycomore trees, and the LORD took me from following the flock, and the LORD said to me, 'Go, prophesy to my people Israel.'" (Amos 7:14-15, NRSV)

What did Amos mean by this? What was this profession of "prophet" that he disowned?

2

Who Were the Prophets?

At first, it sounded like a conventional love song. The singer, plucking the strings of his lyre or harp, began:
"Let me sing for my beloved
my love-song concerning his vineyard:
My beloved had a vineyard
on a very fertile hill..." (Isa 5:1)
In the culture of ancient Israel the word "vineyard" was often just as much associated with romantic love as words like "June" and "moon" are today. The song goes on to describe the care the singer's "beloved" took with his vineyard: preparing the ground, planting choice vines and preparing the vat to store the grapes. But the produce is disappointing. The grapes are useless for making wine – no better than wild grapes.

As with many songs, the logical progression is not obvious. At the beginning it seems to be about the singer's "beloved" who had a vineyard, but then it switches to the first person, and it is the owner of the vineyard who is speaking. And, again as with many songs, his reaction is not entirely rational. A normal vintner would surely ask himself what went wrong. Was the soil not good? Was the position unsuitable? Did he choose the wrong variety of plants, or was there something wrong with the way he planted them? But this is not meant to be a story about the technique of vine growing. This vintner is actually offended and angry with his vineyard. He threatens to take away its hedge and leave it defenceless, to be overgrown with briers and thorns. When he goes on to say, "I will also command the clouds that they rain no rain upon it" it becomes obvious that this is not literally a story about a bad grape harvest. It is the passionate outburst of a spurned lover.

But then it moves into yet another dimension. The tone becomes more challenging, and the listeners suddenly realise that it is not just a love song. It goes on:

"For the vineyard of the LORD of hosts
is the house of Israel,
and the people of Judah
are his pleasant planting."

The lover is God, and the "vineyard" that disappoints him is the nation of Israel. The image of Israel as a vine or a vineyard was also well known. The bad fruit being produced instead of choice grapes is now spelt out:

"he expected justice,
but saw bloodshed;
righteousness,
but heard a cry!"

In the original Hebrew there is a dramatic juxtaposition of similar words: "justice" is *mishpat*, "bloodshed" is *mishpach*; "righteousness" is *ts^edakah* and "a cry" is *ts^e'aqah*, a harsh guttural word to end what started as a sweet love song. This is a protest song.

This song of Isaiah reminds us of something we tend to forget, that some of the biblical prophets were singers. Isaiah today would be playing a guitar. Another example of a singing prophet is found in the story of the escaping Hebrew slaves miraculously crossing the Red Sea while the Egyptians pursuing them were drowned. Moses' sister, the prophet Miriam, leads the women in dancing, playing tambourines, and singing:

"Sing to the LORD, for he has won a glorious victory;
he has thrown the horses and their riders into the sea." (Ex 15:21)

This is preceded in the Bible by a much longer song attributed to Moses, which seems to be a later composition building on that simple verse.

Another female prophet and singer was Deborah (Judges 5),

who stirred up the rather timid Barak to rally the tribes of Israel against oppression by the Canaanites. She and Barak celebrated the victory with a song. Later we hear Samuel describing to Saul "a group of prophets... playing harps, drums, flutes and lyres... dancing and shouting" (1 Sam 10:5). They are in a state of ecstasy: when Saul joins them he becomes "a different person". The prophet Elisha (2 Kings 3:15), when asked for advice in a crisis, called for a musician, and it was as the musician played the harp that the inspiration came on him to utter a prophecy. The later prophets may well have continued the same tradition.

In addition to preaching and singing, some of the prophets had other ways of conveying their message. They practised a kind of street theatre. Isaiah is said to have gone about naked for three years as a sign of the humiliation that was to come on Egypt and Ethiopia (Isa 20). Some of Ezekiel's actions were quite weird and complex. He made a model of the city of Jerusalem under siege, and lay on his side for hundreds of days, cooking his food on cow dung and rationing his water as a sign of the hardship that was to come. He shaved off all his hair and did strange, symbolic things with it to represent what would happen to the nation (Ezek 4-5). At another time, he packed a bundle of his belongings and played out the actions of a refugee. Then he trembled while he ate his food, as a sign of the coming terror (Ezek 12:1-20). At a greater personal cost, he relates how God commanded him not to mourn the death of his wife, so that he could reinforce the message that Jerusalem would lose its pride and joy with no chance to mourn (Ezek 24:15-24). Jeremiah too had felt called to remain unmarried and have no children, as a sign that family life would be destroyed by the coming disaster. He refused to enter a house of mourning or to take part in any customs associated with death, as a sign that in the future there would be so many deaths that there would be no time or opportunity to mourn them (Jer 16:1-9).

Whether singers and actors or not, the prophets were certainly poets. Most of their sayings are in poetic form. In the original Hebrew there is often rhyme, rhythm and alliteration, but this of course is not recognisable when translated into English. Fortunately, however, there is one very common characteristic of Hebrew poetry that is easily transferable to other languages: its parallelism. Parallelism is a kind of rhyming of *ideas*. In practically every verse of Hebrew poetry the second half matches, balances or expands the first half. To take an example from one of the better-known passages in Isaiah:

"For out of Zion shall go forth the law, and the word of the LORD from Jerusalem. And he shall judge among the nations, and shall rebuke many people: and they shall beat their swords into plowshares, and their spears into pruninghooks: nation shall not lift up sword against nation, neither shall they learn war any more." (Isa 2:3-4)

Notice how each thought is repeated in different words or expanded in some way. Wherever we see this pattern in the Bible we can recognise it as poetry. It is present in virtually all the Psalms and in large sections of the prophetic books. The above quotation is from the Authorised Version, which makes it all look like prose, but in most modern versions of the Bible passages like this are arranged in poetic lines.

Poets are sensitive people who feel things very deeply and write with passion. Unlike most ordinary people, they cannot just shrug their shoulders and say "that's life". They have visions that most of us think are unrealistic, and nightmares we would rather not think about. What they write is not meant to be taken in a literal, matter-of-fact way: we are meant to feel the poet's passion and let it move us rather than try too hard to follow the logic of it. Poetry is sometimes difficult to understand, and when we do understand it we may find it uncomfortable. We appreciate the books of the prophets best by realising this. The very last thing we should do is to take them as straightforward instructions or information from God, or use them to "prove" a doctrine or establish an ethical rule. That is not what they are about.

Their books too have something of the nature of an anthology. Each book was put together by a final editor, and patterns and developing themes can be discerned in them. But the order is not usually chronological, and for the ordinary reader today there is seldom a clear "plot" to follow. The best way to read them is to treat them as we would an anthology of poetry, browsing through them and giving our whole attention to one poem at a time.

The prophets were dealing with serious issues. Like all fighters for justice, they were earnest and often angry. But just like fighters for justice today, they knew the strength that can be found in song to raise people's courage and to express the hope that the fight will not be in vain. People who take part in demonstrations and marches hold up banners and shout slogans, but they also sing. The biblical prophets, with all their anger and longing for change, had a faith that made them ultimately confident in the future. They could have said with Martin Luther King, "The arc of the moral universe is long, but it bends towards justice". So as we read them we are invited not just to listen and try to work out what they are saying, but first to share their hope and sing with them.

Why then did Amos deny the label of "prophet"? Just like today, the word in the biblical culture could mean a number of things. "Prophets" or "seers" were often the sort of people that are designated today by the term "shaman". They were people who were thought to have a special relationship with the spirit world. Through various rituals, music, dancing and possibly sometimes drugs, they would go into a trance or an altered state of consciousness. In that state they would enter other realms and dimensions, to communicate with spirits – or, in the case of Israelites, the LORD and his angels – and bring back messages. They could be healers, channels of information that would be otherwise unknown, and foretellers of the future. They often made their living by fortune-telling, giving advice to individuals who came to them. They could also bless people or curse them. Often they belonged to itinerant communities on the fringe of society. The leader of such a community would be called its "father", so that sometimes the whole profession would be called "sons of the prophets". This is probably what Amos meant by saying he was not a prophet's son: he did not belong to that kind of community.

Some prophets were more "establishment" figures, attached to the royal court as advisers to the king. In some ways their situation was like that of the Poet Laureate in Britain, expected to produce poems for important royal and national occasions. Take for instance those words in the Book of Isaiah that are familiar to us from Handel's *Messiah* and Christmas carol services:

"For unto us a child is born, unto us a son is given: and the government shall be upon his shoulder: and his name shall be called Wonderful, Counsellor, The mighty God, The everlasting Father, the Prince of Peace..." (Isa 9:6, AV)

In its original setting this was probably a song to celebrate the birth of a royal prince. Its extravagant expressions, even *"the mighty God"*, were part of the stock language of homage to a king in ancient Middle Eastern culture. But unlike a Poet Laureate today, the court prophet was believed to be able to make things actually happen by the power of his words. One of his chief functions was to help bring victory in war by blessing the army and cursing the enemy. The itinerant prophets who were not part of the royal court often had a similar function.

Another aspect of the function of a prophet appears in the one story in which Abraham is called a prophet. It is a rather strange little story. In the process of his wanderings Abraham visits Gerar, in the southern part of Canaan. He is afraid that because his wife Sarah is so beautiful someone may kill him in order to marry her, and so he passes her off as his sister. Abimelech, the king of Gerar, takes her as a concubine, and God appears to him in a dream and warns him that he will suffer because he has committed the sin of adultery. When Abimelech pleads ignorance, God instructs him to take her back to Abraham because "he is a prophet, and he will pray for you, so that you will not die". (Gen 20:7)

Setting aside the dubious morality of the story, and the fact that it appears three times in different forms (see Gen 12:12-20; 26:6-16), the interesting thing about it from the point of view of prophecy is that the function of a prophet is here seen not as preaching but as intercession.

This comes to the fore in the story of Abraham's intercession for Sodom (Gen 18:22-33). It begins with a soliloquy in the mind of God:

"I will not hide from Abraham what I am going to do… I have chosen him in order that he may command his sons and his descendants to obey me and to do what is right and just…"

We then find Abraham (in the words of NRSV) "standing before the LORD". Abraham opens the conversation by raising the question: what if not all the people of Sodom are deserving of punishment? If, for instance, there are fifty righteous men in the city, will God destroy the righteous along with the wicked? God responds by promising that he will spare the whole city if he finds fifty righteous men in it. Then Abraham embarks on a process very much like the haggling in an Eastern market. What if there are forty-five? And what if there are only forty? Or twenty? Or ten? When Abraham has "beaten him down" to ten, God walks away: that is his final offer. From the subsequent account, it seems that not even ten righteous men could be found. The whole city was destroyed and only Abraham's nephew Lot and his two daughters escaped.

This part of a prophet's role is very prominent in the portrayal of Moses. As he leads the people out of Egypt and through the desert, he is constantly in conversation with God and interceding for the people. He argues in their defence when God is angry and wants to destroy them, and God yields to his pleas and spares them (Ex 32:11-13, 31-32).

Moses is only occasionally called a prophet, notably at the very end of his story, where it is said that "there has never been a prophet in Israel like Moses; the LORD spoke with him face to face" (Deut 34:10). Moses is said to have promised that after his time God "will send you a prophet like me from among your own people, and you are to obey him" (Deut 18:15). This was taken by some people in later times as referring to one special prophet. Muslims see it as a prediction of the prophet Mohammed. However, in all probability it was not meant to refer to one person. It was simply a reassurance that after Moses' time the people would not be left without guidance because God would always provide a prophet. The whole Jewish religion came to be summarised as "the Law and the prophets". The law came through Moses, and this little statement seems meant to establish the relationship between those two pillars of the Jewish faith.

The Israelites in the land of Canaan were at first a league of tribes led by "judges" who emerged from time to time. Their story is told in the book of that name. Some of them were literally judges to whom people resorted when there was a dispute, and who to some extent acted as political leaders. Others were charismatic warrior leaders who emerged in a time of crisis and led the people to victory. Some, it seems, were a combination of both.

The last of the "judges" was Samuel. The Bible begins his story by telling how his mother, who had long prayed for a child, dedicated him to the service of the temple at Shiloh. It goes on to tell the story of how he heard a voice calling his name at night, and thought it was the old priest Eli. Eventually Eli realised it was God who was speaking to the boy, and taught him how to respond (1 Sam 3). This has often been read as a rather charming children's story, but its main point is far from charming. The message Samuel received was that the temple at Shiloh was about to be destroyed because of the corrupt practices of Eli's priestly sons. This happened shortly afterwards, and from then on Samuel was recognised as a prophet. He became the acknowledged leader of the people. Towards the end of his life he reluctantly presided over their transition from a league of tribes to a unified kingdom, but he promised that he would never cease to exercise his prophetic role of interceding for them (1 Sam 12:23). It was he who appointed the first king, Saul, and when Saul fell into disfavour it was Samuel who secretly anointed David as the future king.

So, in the case of Moses and of Samuel, the prophet's function of intercession was closely associated with that of leadership. Once Israel became a kingdom, some prophets filled the role of advisers to the king. But they were not all uncritical supporters of the king. Some of them, at great risk to themselves, stood up to their kings and faced them with unwelcome truth.

An early example of this is the rather amusing story of Balaam (Num 22-24). At the time when the Israelites were reaching the end of their desert wanderings and coming into the land of Canaan, King Balak of Moab, one of the neighbouring countries, was fearful that the Israelites were going to overrun his country, and so he sent for Balaam to curse them. Balaam lived quite far away, near the Euphrates, but was obviously a renowned seer or spell-caster whose words had been proved to be effective. He seems to have been unaware of the Israelite people and yet a worshipper of their God: this is probably the result of the merging or editing of more than one version of the story. Balak sent messengers to Balaam with "the payment for the curse". His first response was to refuse, saying, "Go back home; the LORD has refused to let me go with you". However, when approached for a second time he said that the LORD had given him permission to come, but he could only say what the LORD told him to say. The story then says that the LORD sent an angel to interrupt his journey. Balaam did not see the angel, but his donkey did, and kept turning off the road. Balaam beat the donkey each time this happened, but eventually it lay down under him and refused to move. Balaam was very angry, whereupon the donkey suddenly acquired the gift of human speech and spoke up in its own defence! Eventually Balaam arrived and, after much ritual and offering of sacrifices, he opened his mouth and uttered not a curse on the Israelites but a blessing, accompanied by an oracle prophesying the downfall not only of Moab but of a few other nations as well. This tale, which became part of the folklore of Israel, was at the same time shaped to express the faith that prophets and seers with all their power cannot frustrate the will of Israel's God, the LORD.

Later in the Bible story we find Elijah presented as a powerful "man of God" whom King Ahab hated but at the same time feared. Ahab once greeted Elijah with the words, "So there you are – the worst troublemaker in Israel!" Elijah responded, "I'm not the troublemaker...You are – you and your father. You are disobeying the LORD's commands." (1 Kings 18:17-18).

An exemplary story of a prophet who was willing to "speak truth to power" is that of Micaiah (1 Kings 22), a contemporary of Elijah. Ahab, king of Israel, was trying to draw Jehoshaphat, king of Judah, into a war against the Arameans (Syria). Jehoshaphat said that they should first consult the prophets. They summoned four hundred prophets who all did their professional duty by assuring them that the campaign would be victorious. Jehoshaphat, still doubtful, asked whether there were any other prophets in Israel. Ahab said there was one more, Micaiah, "but I hate him, because he never prophesies anything good for me; it's always something bad". Jehoshaphat insisted that Micaiah should be called. The messenger who was sent for him told him that all the other prophets had predicted success, to which Micaiah responded, "By the living LORD I promise that I will say what he tells me to!" When he came into the presence of the two kings he at first pretended to go along with what the other prophets had said, but Ahab insisted on an honest answer. Micaiah then warned them that such a campaign would be utterly disastrous. He had seen a vision of the LORD decreeing that a deceitful spirit should be sent among the prophets to incite the king to his doom. Ahab said something like "I told you so" and got Micaiah put in prison for his pains. The campaign went ahead, Ahab was killed and the army scattered in disarray.

In a story like this we can see that the prophets were not unquestioningly accepted as vehicles of the word of God. They did not agree with one another. There was much talk of "false prophets", and those later recognised as true prophets were usually in the minority. Their preaching was controversial, and only time would tell who was right.

3

In Their Time and After Their Time

The history in which the prophets are set can be confusing. Their books are not entirely in chronological order, and some of the earlier prophets do not have books named after them: their stories are told in the narrative books earlier in the Bible. The purpose of this chapter is to give the reader some idea of the place of the various prophets in history. However, as we shall see later, this by no means tells the whole story.

The first person in the Bible story to be called a prophet is Abraham, the ancestor of all the Israelites and, in Muslim tradition, the Arabs too. As we have seen, he is only once called a prophet, but the story of his intercession for Sodom presents him as very much a prophetic figure. Next comes Moses, also only occasionally called a prophet, and his sister Miriam. We have also already seen Balaam, a professional prophet from outside the nation of Israel, Deborah, from the days of the "judges", and Samuel, who presided over the transition of Israel from a league of tribes to a kingdom. By this time we have moved from rather undefined ancient times into a history that can be (approximately at least) dated: Samuel was active sometime around 1000 BC.

King David (c 1010-970 BC) had the prophet Nathan as his adviser. His son Solomon seems not to have had a court prophet: the story tells us that on at least two occasions God communicated directly with him in a dream (1 Kings 3:4-15; 9:1-9). After Solomon's death (c 930 BC) there was a civil war in which the kingdom was divided into two: the northern kingdom of Israel, with its capital eventually in Samaria, and the southern kingdom of Judah centred in Jerusalem.

For the next two hundred years or so we hear much more of

prophets in Israel than in Judah. Israel is the setting for the stories of Elijah and Elisha (c 870-850 BC), who were remembered as miracle workers and leaders of itinerant bands of prophets. Micaiah too was active around that time. In the next century, during the comparatively prosperous reign of Jeroboam II (786-746 BC) we find Hosea preaching in Israel and Amos coming to Israel from Judah.

From about 740 BC the focus shifts from Israel to Judah. This is the period of Isaiah and Micah. At this time the Assyrian Empire was growing into the biggest empire that part of the world had yet seen. In about 722 BC it invaded the kingdom of Israel, deported many of its inhabitants and brought in people from elsewhere, thus virtually wiping Israel off the map. It also occupied most of Judah, besieging Jerusalem for a while, but Jerusalem survived. The prophet Isaiah is a key figure in the story of that time.

In the following century Assyria's power waned, and Judah enjoyed a brief period of freedom and prosperity, particularly under the rule of the reforming king Josiah (c 640-609 BC). At that time Zephaniah preached a message mainly of warning, while Nahum rejoiced in the coming destruction of the Assyrian capital, Nineveh, which eventually fell to the Babylonians in 612 BC.

Babylon now became an empire even bigger than that of the Assyrians. The prophet Habakkuk expressed the people's fears about it. The great prophet of this period was Jeremiah, who saw the imminent Babylonian conquest and destruction of Jerusalem as a judgment the people must accept. In 597 BC the Babylonians looted Jerusalem, deported many of its people to Babylon, and set up a puppet king, Zedekiah. After a few years Zedekiah rebelled and in 586 BC the Babylonians under Nebuchadnezzar destroyed Jerusalem and deported many more of its citizens. Ezekiel lived through this time and was among those deported. The stories in the Book of Daniel are set in this time, though as we shall see the book as we now have it belongs to a much later period.

Around 540 BC Babylon was taken over by King Cyrus of the Medes, who became ruler of the even bigger Persian Empire, which came to embrace about half the population of the world at that time. Cyrus introduced a new kind of empire: rather than destroying nations and deporting their populations to the centre, his policy was to enable the various subject peoples to live peacefully, cultivating their own land, worshipping their own gods and practising their own customs. This created the opportunity for Jews in Babylon to return to Judah, rebuild Jerusalem and re-establish themselves as a religious community. The prophet behind Isaiah 40-55 rejoiced in this new beginning, even hailing Cyrus as "the LORD's anointed".

The rebuilding of the temple began, urged on by Haggai and Zechariah, who both preached about 521 BC. It is to this period that the last chapters of Isaiah (56-66) probably belong.

After this time the chronology is uncertain. The consecutive narrative part of the Hebrew Scriptures virtually ends with the Babylonian exile, and we see the history through separate stories such as those of Ezra, Nehemiah and Esther. Most scholars think that the second half of Zechariah (chapters 9-14) also belongs to a later time, probably in the 400s BC. By this time there were numerous Jews living not only in Judea but in other places too. The prophets Obadiah, Joel and Malachi probably belong to this period, but are difficult to date. The Book of Jonah also belongs there: it is not a book of prophecies as such, but a fictional story about a prophet who lived much earlier, long before the Exile (see 2 Kings 14:25).

Persian rule in Judah was replaced about 330 BC by the conquests of Alexander the Great. After his death the areas he had conquered were divided into several kingdoms, but Greek, usually called "Hellenistic", culture became dominant all over the Middle East.

The Book of Daniel is the latest book in the Jewish canon: in fact Jews do not count it among the "prophets" at all but among the miscellaneous "writings" that make up the third section of the Scriptures. It is mainly the kind of literature described as "apocalyptic": a series of cryptic messages cast in the form of dreams, meant to encourage people facing severe persecution. The second half of Zechariah has something of this character about it, and the best known biblical book of this genre is the New Testament Book of Revelation. Daniel belongs to a time in the 160s BC, when a Hellenistic king of Syria was threatening to destroy the Jewish way of life altogether. This led to the Maccabean revolt, which brought in a period of precarious Jewish independence that ended when Judea became part of the Roman Empire in 63 BC.

While this brief overview of the history helps us to see the prophets in their different settings and circumstances, it is by no means the whole story. We have to weigh it against the fact that all the books of the prophets went through a process of re-editing and adaptation over a long period of time. The reason why the sayings of the prophets were preserved at all was that they were found to be relevant in later situations. Things they had predicted had turned out to be true, or the warnings and encouragement they had given to the people were found to be as much needed at a later time as when they were first uttered. As the sayings were repeated by word of mouth, or written and re-written, they were naturally re-worded and adapted to new situations.

Another feature of this process was that people would sometimes add to the words of an earlier prophet, inspired by his spirit and saying what they thought he might have said if he had been living in their time. This means that we cannot assume that any book is entirely the work of the prophet named in the title.

This is most obvious in the case of Isaiah. The book begins:

"The vision of Isaiah son of Amoz, which he saw concerning Judah and Jerusalem in the days of Uzziah, Jotham, Ahaz and

Hezekiah, kings of Judah."

Isaiah's vision in the Temple (Isa 6), which seems to be the story of his call to be a prophet, is said to have happened "in the year that King Uzziah died", which is estimated as 742 or 740 BC. Chapters 36 to 39 of the book are a historical narrative almost identical to the one in the main history (2 Kings 18-20). It tells the story of how the Assyrians, having already destroyed the northern kingdom, laid siege to the city of Jerusalem, and how the prophet Isaiah encouraged King Hezekiah to stand firm and not surrender or look to Egypt for help. Hezekiah took the advice, and there was a miraculous deliverance: some kind of plague hit the Assyrian army and vast numbers of them died in the course of one night. This event can be dated about 701 BC because it is mentioned in Assyrian records – though naturally in a version much more favourable to Assyria! We can thus date Isaiah's prophetic activity in a fairly clear period of about forty years.

But from the beginning of Chapter 40 we find ourselves in a different period altogether. The Assyrians are no longer in the picture. They have been replaced by the Babylonians, who themselves are now being taken over by the Medes. Jerusalem has long since been destroyed and Jewish people have lived for many years in exile in Babylon. The prophet behind this part of the book is rejoicing in the imminent prospect of their return to rebuild the city. The chief instrument in this, Cyrus King of the Medes, is actually mentioned by name (Isa 44:28; 45:1). This was the situation in about 539 BC, about a hundred and sixty years after the Assyrian attack on Jerusalem. This part of the book is evidently the work of a later prophet that came to be included in the Book of Isaiah.

At the beginning of chapter 56 the setting seems to have changed again. The returned exiles are now settled in Judah, and these chapters are concerned with the new problems they are facing. This final part of the book seems to have been produced about twenty years later, and has a mood and style quite different from chapters 40-55.

The joining of these three books into one was not accidental. Although they were evidently produced by different people at different times, there are common themes that run through the whole book. The most obvious one is that all three of them are very much concerned with the city of Jerusalem. The original Isaiah lived in Jerusalem and guided its citizens through challenging times. The prophet behind chapters 40-55 rejoiced in the return of the exiles to Jerusalem to rebuild it, and the one behind chapters 56-66 was concerned with the city's immediate problems and at the same time looked to the glorious "new Jerusalem" that God was going to create. It looks as if those responsible for the later sections meant them as appendices or sequels to the original prophecies of Isaiah. They were saying what they thought Isaiah might have said were he still alive, and that is probably the reason why they are anonymous. They did not see themselves as original authors, but believed that the spirit of Isaiah was speaking through them.

The Book of Isaiah is in fact even more complex than that. Even within the first part of Isaiah there are passages that seem to belong to a later time. Chapter 35 is much closer to the style and mood of chapters 40-55, and seems to have been inserted there by an editor with his own ideas about developing the theme of the whole book. There are other passages in the first part of Isaiah that seem to belong to the period of the second part, notably the graphic depiction of the fall of Babylon (Isa 13-14). In short, the whole Book of Isaiah as we now have it is the result of repeated adaptation and re-working over a period of several centuries.

This composite structure, which is obvious in the Book of Isaiah, is probably true of most of the other books. What we now have in the Bible is basically a collection of writings that reached their final form much later than the events they record. The main turning-point was the Exile. When King Nebuchadnezzar's army destroyed Jerusalem in 586 BC and deported most of its leading citizens to Babylon it appeared that the people of Judah had lost all the pillars of their faith: the Temple they had regarded as the dwelling place of God on earth, the king descended from David who had been promised an everlasting dynasty, and the "land flowing with milk and honey" into which God had led them. As they had been slaves in Egypt, so now they were enslaved in a foreign land again.

In this life-threatening situation for their nation and their faith, some of the Jews found that there were still elements of their way of life that they could maintain in the absence of king, temple or priest. They still had the commandments. They could still pray, and in spite of their servile status in Babylon they could still often practise their distinctive dietary laws and observe the Sabbath. And even more important than these, they still had their *story*. If they were to maintain their faith and way of life, the story had to be remembered and passed on to their children, but it also had to be re-interpreted so that they could find some meaning in what happened.

In this situation some of them looked back to those prophets who had faced the people with their faults, called upon them to change their ways, and preached a God who might judge and chastise but could also forgive. The prophets' words were now collected together, mulled over and adapted to the new situation. The whole history of the nation was written, or re-written, with a view to understanding what had happened and asserting that God was in it all. The books of Joshua, Judges, Samuel and Kings are really an extended sermon about the ways of God with his people, with the history providing the illustrations. That is why in the Jewish Bible these books are included in the section called "the prophets". They are history written by people steeped in the tradition of the prophets.

And so although the Hebrew Bible consists of a number of

different writings produced at different times there is also a sense in which it is one book. All the ancient writings have been worked over and placed in order in accordance with the beliefs of the Jews after the Exile and their interpretation of history. Alteration, re-arranging and addition were an essential part of this process. The prophets in their varied situations, with their varied messages, have been woven together into the "big story" of Israel and its relationship with its God.

Jesus inherited this "big story" and its Scriptures but, like some of the prophets before him, challenged it and changed it. He too was a poet: see for instance the Beatitudes (Matt 5:3-10). He was a passionate preacher, a satirist and a humourist. He echoed the way in which Amos and Isaiah made justice a priority and religious practices secondary, as in his challenge:

"So if you are about to offer your gift at the altar and there you remember that your brother has something against you, leave your gift there in front of the altar, go at once and make peace with your brother, and then come back and offer your gift to God." (Matt 5:23-24).

Centuries of Christian tradition have taught us to see Jesus in a rather "churchy" way and to see the Old Testament prophets as merely predicting things about him. To read the prophets as people of their own times in their own unique situations, and then to read the Gospels, can give us a deeper sense of Jesus as part of that rich prophetic tradition. It can help us to see how he brought a fresh, challenging revival of that tradition and at the same time a transformation and fulfilment of it.

The early Christians kept the Hebrew Scriptures but also told their own story. And so we have the Christian Bible in two parts, the Old Testament and the New Testament. But these, for Christians, are not really two separate books. The way Christians read the Hebrew Scriptures is different from the way Jews read them. For Christians the New Testament message changes the meaning of the older Scriptures. Those writings that came from many different people and different times and were merged into the faith of Judaism have now been merged into the Christian faith.

The "big story" in a sense is still being written. Jews have re-interpreted it down through the ages in the light of their thought and experience, and Christians in the light of theirs. While the *content* of the Scriptures has now been fixed for many centuries, their *meaning* is still developing. Every new generation has its own concerns and questions which shape its interpretation of them and in a sense create a new story. The sixteenth century monk Martin Luther desperately searched the Bible to find a gracious God who could save him from his sins. In the twentieth century, an American Baptist pastor named after him drew on the Bible for inspiration in the struggle for civil rights for black people, an issue that was not on the agenda at all for his namesake.

In our time we have seen the rise of many quite different ways of reading the Bible. "Base communities" of poor people in South America and other places have learned to read it from the point of view of the underdog and produce a "liberation theology". Women studying the Bible have seen things in it that generations of male scholars never noticed, producing a whole school of biblical interpretation labelled as "feminist". People whose sexuality or gender does not fit the traditional norm have developed "queer" interpretation, and scholars in countries that are striving to escape from the legacy of European empires have developed a "post-colonial" interpretation. Some American writers today see Assyria, Babylon and Rome repeated in the "empire" of global capitalism and read the Bible as a challenge to it.

Some have more eccentric and exclusive ways of interpreting the Bible. Many people read the prophets with the assumption that they contain accurate predictions of the future course of world history. They eagerly compare the biblical prophecies with contemporary events and use them to forecast the future. This too is something that changes with the perspective of time. The first readers of the visions in Daniel 7 probably saw the four evil kingdoms as Assyria, Babylon, Persia and Greece, and believed that the events through which they were living in the 160s BC were the final run up to the establishing of the kingdom of the saints of God. Modern interpreters have seen Islam, Communism or even the Papacy as the last of the four, and assume that the coming of the final kingdom will be in our own time.

Some people see the Bible as revealing mystic wisdom to those who are initiated and can understand the code. This way of reading it has existed in different forms for many centuries. In the Jewish rabbinic tradition the Bible text has been studied in minute detail virtually irrespective of its plain meaning, and some symbolic or allegorical meaning has been found not only in whole passages but in individual words and even letters. In modern times there are individuals who propagate quite eccentric messages by something like this method.

This raises the question: can the Bible mean anything we wish it to mean? We can certainly not *prevent* people from reading it in ways very different from the way we ourselves would read it, and we have to be cautious in dogmatically asserting that our interpretation is the "right" one. But we do have some criteria for judging some interpretations as more sensible than others. There is the *historical* criterion: although we can never be certain of the facts of history, we do have enough information to give us a feel for what is historically likely and we can recognise a gross anachronism when we see one. There are some things that we cannot imagine the prophets knowing or thinking in the time in which they lived.

However, for some methods of reading the Bible, such as the allegorical method in ancient times and some literary approaches today, the historical consideration is not all-important. What is more important for those who value the Bible as Holy Scripture is the *theological* criterion: the Scriptures were developed within a particular tradition of belief, first in the Jewish community and then in the Christian Church. With all their differences, Jews and Christians believe in the same God and recognise God as having a certain character. We can therefore feel free to say that any interpretation of the Bible that is radically contrary to this view of God, even if it is preached by some religious people, is illegitimate.

Bearing this caution in mind, there is nothing to prevent us from reacting to the prophets in new ways. We need not feel bound to the "original" meaning, or obliged to interpret a passage exclusively in the light of its historical background: in spite of all the scholarship available, we are still pretty ignorant of this anyway. Nor should we feel obliged to interpret the prophets within the framework of our theology: that too is culturally conditioned and can change with time. Without exact knowledge of the history, we can let our imagination work on the *kind* of situation that lies behind the words. We can enjoy what is often stirring and sublime poetry. We too can continue what the biblical editors and writers did. We can imaginatively see the prophets' relevance to situations in our own time and so incorporate them in *our* big story, *our* "Bible".

4

A Passion for Justice

Amos was not the first prophet in Israel to preach about social justice. A hundred years before his time, in that same kingdom of Israel, the prophet Elijah had stood up to King Ahab. A man called Naboth had a vineyard adjacent to Ahab's palace, and Ahab wanted to buy it in order to extend his gardens. Naboth refused to sell it. As a faithful Israelite he regarded his small portion of the "Promised Land" as a sacred trust to be kept in his family forever. Ahab was disappointed and angry but (perhaps still influenced by the Israelite values he had inherited) was ready to accept the situation. His wife Jezebel, being of a different culture, had other ideas. She plotted to get Naboth condemned to death on false charges, so that Ahab could "legitimately" take possession of the vineyard. Elijah then faced Ahab with his offence against God and prophesied that Ahab's dynasty would soon collapse (1 Kings 21).

Even further back we have the example of the prophet Nathan. He was for the most part a conventional court prophet, an adviser to King David. It was he who declared God's promise that the dynasty of David would last forever (2 Sam 7). But later he came with a very different message (2 Sam 11-12). David had committed adultery with Bathsheba, the wife of Uriah. Finding that Bathsheba was pregnant, he tried to arrange things so that Uriah would think the child was his own. When this did not work, he secretly arranged to have Uriah "accidentally" killed in battle, and then married Bathsheba. He thought he had got away with it, but Nathan knew what he had done and faced him with it.

The basis of his rebuke is significant. He made his point by telling a story. There was a rich man, he said, who had numerous flocks and herds. In the same town there was a poor man who had just one ewe lamb which he kept as a pet. He would feed it with his own food, let it drink from his cup, and hold it in his lap. One day the rich man needed to provide dinner for an unexpected guest, but instead of slaughtering one of his own animals he stole the poor man's lamb. David was appalled at such wickedness and cried out, "I swear by the living LORD that the man who did this ought to die!" Then Nathan said those famous words, "You are that man!" David had exercised his power as King of Israel, blessed with a number of wives, to steal the beloved only wife of one of his loyal subjects. The interesting thing about this story is that Nathan represented David's action not as the transgression of a sexual taboo but as a matter of justice: David had quite simply acted *unfairly*.

Justice was a central theme for the prophets from early times. It would of course be anachronistic to attribute some kind of social or economic theory to them, or to call them socialists. Their concern sprang from their understanding of Israel's God as a God of righteousness and fair dealing, and from the concept of the nation as a family, the "children of Israel". As members of one family they had a sacred responsibility to care for one another. At the same time the God they believed in was a God of mercy. Their laws told them to care not just for each other but for the stranger and the traveller too. The same chapter of the Book of Leviticus that says, "You shall love your neighbour as yourself" also says, "you shall love the alien as yourself" (Lev 19:18-34).

The prophet Isaiah, who began his activity in Jerusalem a few decades after Amos had preached in the northern kingdom, shared that prophet's passion for justice and his belief that acts of worship were meaningless without it.

The first chapter of Isaiah reads like a kind of rant. The prophet points out the poor, beleaguered state of the nation as its land is occupied by the Assyrians. The city of Jerusalem stands in the middle of a devastated landscape like a shed in a field of cucumbers. The people are saying that were it not for a few survivors it would have been like Sodom and Gomorrah, those ancient cities on the Dead Sea plain which had, according to legend, been destroyed because of their extreme wickedness. Then the prophet turns on the leading citizens of Judah and implies that in fact they are just as bad:

"Hear the word of the LORD,

you rulers of Sodom!

Listen to the teaching of our God,

you people of Gomorrah!" (Isa 1:10, NRSV)

The people could have responded that they were in fact very pious. They had not turned away from God. Crowds still flocked to the temple to pray and offer sacrifices. They scrupulously observed all the ritual and turned out in great numbers for the festivals. But like Amos, Isaiah sees God pouring scorn on all that:

"Do you think I want all these sacrifices you keep offering to me?... Who asked you to do all this tramping about in my temple? It's useless to bring your offerings. I am disgusted with the smell of the incense you burn. I cannot stand your New Moon Festivals, your Sabbaths, and your religious gatherings... When you lift your hands in prayer, I will not look at you..."

And why? Because:

"your hands are covered with blood. Wash yourselves clean."

He was not thinking of the customary ritual washing that is often required before prayer. The cleansing they needed was something much more real, something social and political:

"Stop all this evil that you are doing. Yes, stop doing evil and learn to do right. See that justice is done – help those who are oppressed, give orphans their rights, and defend widows."

Religious people often blame "godlessness" for national decline or misfortune. Today this "godlessness" usually means things like the decline in churchgoing, the growth of liberalism, or a more tolerant attitude to people's sex lives. People often quote the biblical proverb "righteousness exalteth a nation" (Prov 14:34, AV). But it is not often remembered that in the Bible the real meaning of "righteousness" is *justice*: people dealing fairly with one another both as individuals and as classes in society.

Further on, Isaiah pictures God saying to the leaders of the people:

"It is you who have devoured the vineyard;
the spoil of the poor is in your houses.
What do you mean by crushing my people,
by grinding the face of the poor?
says the Lord GOD of hosts." (Isa 3:14-15)

"Grinding the face of the poor" today has become a stock phrase with a rather Dickensian flavour, almost a joke. Most of us ordinary people in the West do not see ourselves reflected in that phrase. The statement that "the spoil of the poor is in your houses" is more challenging for us. When we look at our larders full of imported food, much of it produced by virtual slave labour, our wardrobes full of bargain clothes and our household appliances made in lethally dangerous Asian factories, and the dire poverty in parts of the world that produce the luxuries we enjoy, we need to be reminded of where it all comes from. Much of it has been virtually looted from the poor.

Isaiah talked about the practice of land-grabbing that was already present in his time:

"You buy more houses and fields to add to those you already have. Soon there will be nowhere for anyone else to live, and you alone will live in the land!" (Isa 5:8)

This resonates with so much in history, from the Highland Clearances of the early nineteenth century to the large scale "agribusinesses" of today. Farmers who have cultivated their land for generations are forced out of it to become labourers working for other people's luxuries rather than their own needs, or to migrate to the precarious employment markets of the big cities. Large areas of land in poorer countries (together with the precious resource of water) are taken up with hotels and golf courses for the tourist trade. Rich agricultural land that could produce fruit and vegetables for the local population is dedicated to cash crops for export. Irreplaceable natural forest is used for the ridiculously wasteful process of converting grass into beef steaks.

For Isaiah, the scandal of this land-grabbing process had a particular religious grounding. The land was a basic element in Israel's faith. It was "the Promised Land": God had set the Hebrew slaves free in Egypt, led them through the desert and given them this "land flowing with milk and honey". There was something sacrilegious and offensive to God about selling and buying it as a mere piece of property. One of the laws in the Torah says:

"Your land must not be sold on a permanent basis, because you do not own it; it belongs to God, and you are like foreigners who are allowed to make use of it." (Lev 25:23)

This law comes in the context of the "Jubilee year": every fifty years debts were to be cancelled, slaves set free, and land returned to its original owner. We do not know how often this was actually practised, and certainly once the Jews lost control of their own land it would have been very difficult to implement, but the concept behind it was important.

One of the Psalms declares that "the earth is the LORD's, and all that is in it" (Ps 24:1). This concept of the sacredness of the land is of course not exclusive to the biblical tradition: it is present in many ancient cultures. In the tradition of the native Australians the land was their sacred mother and the idea of individuals *owning* bits of it was unthinkable. In that country too the appropriation of the land into private ownership has had tragic effects on the aboriginal culture.

This greed has consequences:

"I have heard the LORD Almighty say, 'All these big, fine houses will be empty ruins'".

Perhaps what Isaiah had in mind was a devastating foreign invasion that would be God's judgment on the people's greed. Yet we have seen in our own time how when houses and land become mere commodities their natural use falls into the background and they are caught up in the vagaries of the market. Perfectly sound buildings are demolished or left empty. Well-built houses that were once homes to large families are bought by profit-grabbing landlords and divided into apartments and bedsits that end up as slums. Rural communities are destroyed as farmhouses and cottages inhabited by generations of the same family are turned into holiday cottages and stand empty for half the year. People sleep on the streets of big cities while hundreds of dwellings stand unoccupied. Working class city dwellers are forced to move because large scale developers are drawn by the value of the estates they live on.

There is also a hint of the cost of this kind of development in terms of the fertility of the land:

"Five acres of vineyard shall yield only a gallon
And ten bushels of seed return only a peck." (Isa 5:10, REB)

The prophet here is probably thinking of a famine that will come as a judgment on all this greed and injustice. Or perhaps already in his time he had seen something of the consequences of land being bought as an investment. The new owners would not care for the land as its original owners did. Or they might turn it from productive farming to their own private leisure purposes. There is no shortage of examples today of the environmentally disastrous effect of large-scale agriculture oriented to maximum profit and the over-use of artificial fertilisers and pesticides. Whatever the prophet's original meaning, the message is the same: greed does not work.

Isaiah was no stranger to the complicity of government in this exploitation:

"You make unjust laws that oppress my people. That is how you prevent the poor from having their rights and from getting justice. That is how you take the property that belongs to widows and orphans." (Isa 10:1-2)

Injustice is the almost inevitable consequence of great power and the accumulation of wealth. The prophets knew about *hubris* long before the Greek word became familiar in the English language. They sensed that there was something about extreme power and excessive consumption that was incompatible with the nature of Israel as a holy people, and that invited disaster. Isaiah says of Judah:

"Their land is full of silver and gold, and there is no end to their treasures; their land is full of horses, and there is no end to their chariots."

Horse-drawn chariots were characteristic of imperial power rather than a humble people's need to defend itself: they were the equivalent of today's tanks and warships. Not only was the nation accumulating great wealth, but it was involved in an arms race, over-reaching itself and trying to be a great power.

The prophet sees that this cannot last. He sees God planning a day to bring all this to an end:

"When that day comes they will throw away the gold and silver idols they have made, and abandon them to the moles and the bats... people will hide in holes and caves in the rocky hills..." (Isa 2:7,20-21)

One cannot help thinking of the two sharply contrasting aspects of the developed world today. On the one hand there is conspicuous wealth and luxury, and complex systems to enable us to live in safety and freedom, but all this has an under-girding that is actually very fragile. Always lurking in the background are the nightmares of terrorism, nuclear war and climate change. For "holes and caves in the rocky hills" we could easily read "nuclear fall-out shelters".

Isaiah mocked the conspicuous luxury enjoyed by the women

of Jerusalem. One detects a rather male chauvinist tone in this, but we have to admit that in most societies even today a man's wealth and status tend to be judged by how well his wife and daughters are dressed! Isaiah sees the "daughters of Zion" who:

"...walk with outstretched necks,

glancing wantonly with their eyes,

mincing along as they go,

tinkling with their feet"

He foresees a day when the LORD will take away "the finery of the anklets, the headbands, and the crescents, the pendants, the bracelets..." and so on. We get the feeling that Isaiah is having fun here as he makes a list of twenty-one items that could easily be found in the catalogue of an up-market fashion store today. It even includes the suggestion of a "punk" fashion for nose rings! Then comes the shocking description of an end to all this, when these overdressed, perfumed ladies will be destitute and unwashed:

"Instead of perfume there will be a stench,

and instead of a sash, a rope;

and instead of well-arranged hair, baldness;

and instead of a rich robe, a binding of sackcloth;

instead of beauty, shame." (Isa 3:16-24, NRSV)

Isaiah's daring vision saw even the mighty Assyrian Empire as a mere tool in the hands of Israel's God (Isa 10:5-25). The Assyrian invasion of Israel was just a part of God's purpose to chastise his people:

"I use Assyria like a club to punish those with whom I am angry. I sent Assyria to attack a godless nation..."

This, of course, is not how the Emperor himself saw it. The prophet imagines him saying:

"I have done it all myself. I am strong and wise and clever. I wiped out the boundaries between nations and took the supplies they had stored... The nations of the world were like a bird's nest, and I gathered their wealth as easily as gathering eggs. Not a wing fluttered to scare me off, no beak opened to scream at me."

But then comes God's reply:

"Can an axe claim to be greater than the man who uses it? Is a saw more important than the man who saws with it?"

This mighty emperor is only a tool in God's hand! God is using him for the time being to chastise his people, but his own turn will come to face judgment for his arrogance. In attacking Israel he will have Israel's God to deal with, and he will get more than his fingers burnt:

"God, the light of Israel, will become a fire. Israel's holy God will become a flame, which in a single day will burn up everything..."

Isaiah assures the people that Assyria's domination will not last forever:

"The Sovereign LORD Almighty says to his people who live in Zion, 'Do not be afraid of the Assyrians, even though they oppress you as the Egyptians used to do. In only a little while I will finish punishing you, and then I will destroy them."

Micah, a slightly younger contemporary of Isaiah, shared Isaiah's anger about the prevalent injustice. He too denounced the greedy landowners:

"When they want fields, they seize them; when they want houses, they take them. No one's family or property is safe" (Mic 2:2)

He attacked the national leaders:

"You skin my people alive and tear the flesh off their bones. You eat my people up. You strip off their skin, break their bones, and chop them up like meat for the pot." (Mic 3:2-3)

It is Micah who, decrying the extreme sacrifices the people are making in their efforts to appease God, gives us that classic expression of the essence of true religion:

"and what does the LORD require of you
but to do justice, and to love kindness,

and to walk humbly with your God?" (Mic 6:8)

Much later, when the Jews had been exiled in Babylon and had returned to rebuild Jerusalem and establish themselves as a renewed worshipping community, the call for justice seems to have been as necessary as ever. The prophet behind the third part of the Book of Isaiah reacts to the way the people are complaining that God does not honour their fasting and answer their prayers. He points out that even on fast days they are caring only for their own interests and fighting among themselves. He mocks the pious self-humiliation of their fasts, how they bow their heads low "like a blade of grass" and grovel in sackcloth and ashes. He tells them God is saying:

"The kind of fasting I want is this; remove the chains of oppression and the yoke of injustice, and let the oppressed go free. Share your food with the hungry and open your homes to the homeless poor..." (Isa 58)

From the earliest prophets to the latest, the call to justice is crystal clear. But we know that in the real world things are not quite so simple. The achievement of justice is complicated and often controversial. What seems just to some seems unjust to others. The biblical prophets, as we shall see in the next chapter, were not unaware of this.

5

What is Justice?

As the Assyrian Empire was approaching its end, the prophet Nahum produced a little book that is entirely devoted to exulting and gloating over the imminent fall of Nineveh, the Assyrian capital. The prophet revels in the disasters about to come to this city whose oppression has kept Israel under for so long. He sees the runners bringing to Judah the news that Nineveh has fallen:

"Look, a messenger is coming over the mountains with good news! He is on his way to announce the victory! People of Judah, celebrate your festivals... The wicked will never invade your land again." (Nahum 1:15)

This is certainly a book that revels in the destruction of the enemy. Its theme is summed up in its closing words, in which the prophet says to Nineveh:

"All those who hear the news of your destruction clap their hands for joy. Did anyone escape your endless cruelty?" (Nahum 3:19)

In the Book of Isaiah (14:3-23) is a vision of the fall of Babylon, the empire that took over when Assyria collapsed. The prophet pictures long dead kings and conquerors greeting the king of Babylon as he joins them in the underworld:

"The world of the dead is getting ready to welcome the king of Babylon. The ghosts of those who were powerful on earth are stirring about. The ghosts of kings are rising from their thrones. They all call out to him, 'Now you are as weak as we are! You are one of us!... You lie on a bed of maggots and are covered with a blanket of worms.'"

His fate is even worse than that of other kings. They at least had decent burial, but in the case of this king they say:

"All the kings of the earth lie in their magnificent tombs, but you have no tomb, and your corpse is thrown out to rot.'"

This passage includes a familiar sentence, better known in the words of the King James Bible:

"How art thou fallen from heaven, O Lucifer, son of the morning!" (Isa 14:12)

This has been read by some interpreters as referring to the doctrine that the Devil was originally an angel who rebelled against God and was sent down to hell, but such an interpretation takes it right out of its context. Titles like this (translated in the Good News Bible as "bright morning star") were a normal part of the extravagant titles claimed by powerful kings. It is not unlikely that the emperor of Babylon would be perceived by devout Jews as just the kind of blasphemer who would boast of ascending to heaven and raising his throne above the stars.

The theme of the "turning of the tables" is a strong one in the prophets. Their belief in divine justice meant that the victims of injustice would one day have the satisfaction of seeing their former oppressors punished and humiliated. The high would be brought down and the low lifted up. The story of the Exodus set this pattern very firmly in Israelite tradition and folklore: the Egyptian taskmasters and Pharaoh himself struck by plagues until they pleaded with the Hebrew slaves to leave them, and their charioteers drowned in the sea while the slaves crossed over in safety. Later we find the stories of Samson humiliating the Philistines, the young shepherd David killing the giant Goliath, and many others.

The theme continues into the New Testament, especially in the Gospel of Luke, which gives us Mary's song, the Magnificat (Luke 1:46-55), modelled on the song of Samuel's mother Hannah (1 Sam 2:1-10):

"He hath shewed strength with his arm; he hath scattered the proud in the imagination of their hearts. He hath put down the mighty from their seats, and exalted them of low degree. He hath filled the hungry with good things; and the rich he hath sent empty away." (AV)

Luke goes on to quote Jesus saying:

"Happy are you who are hungry now;

you will be filled!

Happy are you who weep now;

you will laugh...

But how terrible for you who are rich now;

You have had your easy life!

How terrible for you who are full now;

you will go hungry!

How terrible for you who laugh now;

you will mourn and weep." (Luke 6:21-25)

Luke also quotes a passage in the third part of Isaiah:

"The spirit of the Lord GOD is upon me,

because the LORD has anointed me;

he has sent me to bring good news to the oppressed,

to bind up the broken-hearted,

to proclaim liberty to the captives,

and release to the prisoners;

to proclaim the year of the LORD's favour,

and the day of vengeance of our God..." (Isa 61:1-2, NRSV;

Luke 4:16-19)

Luke shows Jesus reading these words in the synagogue at
Nazareth as a kind of manifesto of his mission, but "the day of
vengeance" is missing. In Isaiah these words are followed by
even more beautiful expressions like "a garland instead of ashes,
the oil of gladness instead of mourning", but it soon becomes
clear that this is a prophecy of the Jews becoming "top dogs":

"My people, foreigners will serve you.

They will take care of your flocks

And farm your land and tend your vineyards...

You will enjoy the wealth of the nations

And be proud that it is yours." (Isa 61:5-6)

But in Luke's Gospel we find Jesus making himself very

unpopular by commenting on this passage that foreigners have often been more open to receive God's blessings than those who are called God's people.

However, there are already hints in the Book of Isaiah of a more inclusive vision. In the first part of the book, following a dire prophecy of the downfall of the Egyptian Empire, the prophet introduces a new idea (Isa 19:16-25):

"The LORD will reveal himself to the Egyptian people, and then they will acknowledge and worship him... The LORD will punish the Egyptians, but then he will heal them. They will turn to him, and he will hear their prayers and heal them."

Assyria too will be involved in this great conversion. There will be a highway from Egypt to Assyria, and both empires will become one community worshipping the God of Israel. They, together with Israel, will be "a blessing to all the world".

This is a bold vision coming from a prophet in the tiny kingdom of Judah. Yet little did people of that time realise that the time would come when the whole region of Egypt, Palestine and Syria would be united by one faith: first the Christian faith and then Islam, both religions that worship that same God who in Isaiah's time was worshipped in the temple in Jerusalem!

And so, through all the dreams of the underdogs longing to see their oppressors punished and humiliated, there breaks through here and there the much bigger vision already encapsulated in the promise to Abraham that "through you I will bless all the nations" (Gen 12:3). It is the birth of the realisation that justice is not just a matter of the victims of injustice seeing vengeance wreaked on their oppressors, but of things being put right in a much more profound and universal way.

The outworking of divine justice raises another issue. We would all agree that greed and injustice have consequences. A nation or an empire built on injustice and oppression is ultimately doomed to failure. Tyrants are brought down and regimes that seemed impregnable have come to an end. We have seen this happen in recent history: the defeat of Nazi Germany, the collapse of Communist regimes in Eastern Europe, and the ending of dictatorships in many parts of the world. But we know from experience that the process is rarely smooth or peaceful. There is a general feeling of satisfaction that the tyrants have got what they deserve, but in practice many innocent people suffer too. In what way does this show the justice of God?

The story of Abraham's bargaining with God about the fate of Sodom (Gen 18:16-33), as it now stands, may have been shaped by the concerns of later prophets with this question. Abraham asks, "Are you really going to destroy the innocent with the guilty?" and challenges God himself by saying, "The judge of all the earth has to act justly".

This story reminds us of an important feature of many of the prophets. They did not simply teach that God is just: they explored and questioned what that justice meant. They sometimes argued with God and challenged him to keep his promises and act consistently with his true nature. We see this especially in some of the prayers of Moses (e.g., Ex 5:22-23; 32:11-13). Faith, as expressed in the Bible, is not an unquestioning acceptance of revealed truth, but an active attempt to work out the nature of God by puzzling over the way things work in the world. The Jewish prisoners who "put God on trial" in Auschwitz were acting well within the biblical tradition.

The Book of Jonah is one that everybody has heard of but few people know. It has of course been mercilessly mocked, caricatured and argued about. We could say that whether that "great fish" existed or not, we can be certain of its species: it is an enormous red herring! Arguments over it have had the unfortunate effect of diverting attention from a wonderful little book which is humorous, ironic and at the same time one of the most challenging and profound writings in the Hebrew Scriptures.

Uniquely among the prophetic books, it is not a collection of the teachings of a prophet, but a story about a prophet. It is a kind of "what if?" story, tagged onto a prophet of whom virtually nothing was known (2 Kings 14:25) and who could therefore be used as a hypothetical example to raise a disturbing question. The prophets were always preaching about the sins of the Gentile nations, and especially threatening doom to the empires that threatened and oppressed Israel. The Book of Nahum is a prime example of this, referring to Nineveh, the same city featured in Jonah. When the prophets preached judgment on Israel itself, they always included the promise that if the people repented and turned back to God the punishment would be revoked. Their preaching was not unalterable prediction: it was a wake-up call. But they rarely considered whether this applied to the other nations too. What if the other nations actually listened to the prophets of Israel and repented? For most Jews living under the oppression of powerful empires this was unthinkable, but what if it really happened? Would God forgive them too?

And so the writer of this book tells a fictional, partly allegorical, story of a prophet called Jonah who, instead of preaching within Israel and threatening judgment on other nations far away, was actually called to go and preach directly to the people of Nineveh, the capital of the ruthlessly oppressive Assyrian empire. As if to make it quite clear that the story is fictional and hypothetical, the writer includes comically exaggerated elements: a man swallowed by an enormous fish and living inside it for three days, God speaking to a fish, a city so big it would take three days to cross it, and cattle in the fields wearing sackcloth and praying!

Suppose a prophet heard the call of God to go and preach in Nineveh. His first reaction would be not to do it. Apart from its being very dangerous, he would inevitably doubt whether it was a proper thing for an Israelite prophet to do: they were supposed to be God's messengers to his people Israel, not to the Gentile nations who did not know him. Would a foreign nation recognise the authority of Israel's God and take the message seriously anyway? And so, in the story, Jonah responds to the summons by going off in the opposite direction. We are not quite sure where Tarshish was, but it is thought to have been a city on the south coast of what is now Spain – virtually the other end of the world for ancient Israelites. His intention – a flat contradiction of his faith – was to get as far away from Israel's God as possible.

Before long a fierce storm blew up and threatened to sink the ship. The foreign sailors cried out each to their own god. They threw as much cargo as possible overboard to lighten the load. Jonah meanwhile was down in his cabin, fast asleep. They woke him and demanded that he too should pray to whatever god he worshipped. They presumed that the storm had been brought on by some god who had a quarrel with one of the people on board. They used their usual method of divination to find out who it was, and it turned out to be Jonah. When they tried to get more information about him, he made the statement that all Jewish people were proud to stand up and make: "I am a Hebrew... I worship the LORD, the God of heaven, who made land and sea". Then he immediately contradicted himself by telling them he was running away from this God by taking to the sea! To give him some credit, he then invited them to throw him off the boat, but they, to their credit, tried hard to get to the nearest shore. When they eventually realised there was no other way, they prayed to Jonah's God that he would not hold this action against them, and threw him overboard, at which the storm immediately ceased.

So, while the prophet of the true God was floundering in the sea, these heathen sailors were offering a sacrifice and making vows to Israel's God. Here there was already an indication that Gentiles were as able to respond to God as any Jew. Jonah was then swallowed by a great fish. Uncomfortable as it was, it saved his life, and so he prayed and sang a psalm of thanksgiving in the belly of the fish. Then the fish vomited him out onto dry land, not because it could no longer tolerate having an indigestible singing prophet in its stomach, but because the LORD had told it to!

The opening of the third chapter is a simple and beautiful expression of divine forgiveness: "Once again the LORD spoke to Jonah…" – and this time he obeyed. We then have the sum total of the message that Jonah preached as a prophet: "In forty days Nineveh will be destroyed!" It seems that in response to this, with no further persuasion or questioning of Jonah's credentials, the people started fasting and putting on sackcloth. When the king heard of this, he himself put on sackcloth and covered himself in ashes, and issued a proclamation that all his subjects, and even the sheep, goats and cattle throughout the kingdom should do the same, give up their evil ways and pray to God for mercy. The result was that God changed his mind, and so Jonah's prophecy that Nineveh would be destroyed in forty days was no longer true.

Jonah's reaction at this point was something like "why am I not surprised?" He told the LORD that he had known all along that he was "a loving and merciful God, always patient, always kind, and always ready to change your mind and not punish". That was why he had not gone to Nineveh the first time: he did not want to be the instrument of Nineveh repenting and being spared. He was now extremely angry, so angry that he prayed to die.

It is at this point that we can begin to see the real seriousness of the book. Preachers sometimes portray Jonah as just a stuffy self-righteous prig, and assume the humour in the book is intended as satire. But why was he actually suicidal? Is that just another comic exaggeration? To answer this, we have to remember what Nineveh meant in the memory of Jewish people. Often we think of "sinners" as people whose way of life the pious disapprove of. But in the mind of the ancient Jews the Assyrians were not "sinners" in that tame sense. Nineveh was the capital of an oppressive empire that had been responsible for untold bloodshed and cruelty. It had destroyed the kingdom of

Israel, overrun most of Judah and laid siege to Jerusalem itself. At the time the book was probably written this was history, but its readers would have had recent experience of similar oppression under the Babylonians. The question being raised is: would God ever forgive this arch enemy of his people? The very suggestion of such a thing would be as disturbing to Jews of that time as would be the suggestion to modern Jews that the Nazis could just apologise for the Holocaust and be forgiven. This is why Jonah wanted to die: he could not face living in a world where people could get away with such wickedness just by repenting. If this was how God ran the world, he wanted out.

The book ends not with a dogmatic statement but with a gentle dialogue between God and Jonah about a bush that dies, and then a question:

"And should I not be concerned about Nineveh, that great city, in which there are more than a hundred and twenty thousand people who do not know their right hand from their left, and also many animals?" (Jonah 4:11, NRSV)

This little book, with its intentional humour in some parts and its unintentional funniness to modern ears in other parts, raises an enormous question: the question of the scandalous forgiveness of God that goes so far beyond justice as sometimes to seem unjust. At the same time it opens up an incredible vision of God's intimate and universal love that reaches to his humblest creatures both human and animal. And, by ending with a question mark, it suggests that the conversation is not yet closed.

In this it anticipates some of the parables of Jesus, like the one about the prodigal son and his elder brother, or the workers in the vineyard who all got the same whether their hours were long or short (Luke 15:11-32; Matt 20:1-16). The complaint of the vineyard workers, like that of the prodigal son's elder brother, is suggestive of the discontent of many people today. People who have worked hard all their lives, paid their taxes and accumulated savings often feel quite justified in their resentment as they see those who have been lazy or less prudent, or who have just arrived in the country, being looked after by the welfare state at their expense.

In the real world the working out of what is truly fair is never simple: it is often controversial and very emotive. The biblical writers wrestled with this question as much as we do. They wondered why God seems sometimes to punish the innocent along with the guilty and at other times to reward the guilty as much as the innocent. In books like Jonah and in the teaching of Jesus the unconditional compassion and forgiveness of God has an element of scandal about it.

6

The Battle of the Cults

One of the traditional favourites in children's Bible story books is the story of Elijah's contest with the prophets of Baal on Mount Carmel (1 Kings 18:20-40). King Ahab's foreign wife Jezebel was an enthusiast for the worship of Baal and his consort Asherah, and she was actively persecuting the prophets of the God of Israel. Elijah challenged the Baal prophets to a great test. He and they were each to prepare a bull for a burnt offering and, instead of lighting the fire themselves, pray to their god to send fire down from heaven. The story is built up in highly dramatic and satirical terms. The Baal prophets prayed all day, doing their ritual dances around the altar and cutting themselves with swords and lances, but nothing happened. Elijah stood by and mercilessly mocked them:

"Pray louder! He is a god! Maybe he is daydreaming or relieving himself, or perhaps he's gone on a journey! Or maybe he's sleeping, and you've got to wake him up!"

Finally they gave up, and Elijah rebuilt the old altar of the LORD that was nearby, laid a bull on it and drenched the carcass, the wood and the whole altar with water. He prayed to the LORD to display his power, and a sudden fire came down from the sky and consumed the lot – even the stone altar! All the people cried out, "The LORD indeed is God! The LORD indeed is God!" The children's version of the story does not always include the next sentence, which says that Elijah then incited the people to slaughter all the four hundred and fifty prophets of Baal.

This battle of the cults was the context of virtually all the prophets in ancient Israel. Those whom the biblical writers regarded as the true prophets were fighting for the pure worship of the LORD against the worship of other gods. The principle is laid down in the first two of the Ten Commandments:

"Worship no god but me.

Do not make for yourselves images of anything in heaven or on earth or in the water under the earth. Do not bow down to any idol or worship it, because I am the LORD your God and I tolerate no rivals." (Ex 20:3-5)

The battle commences almost immediately. As Moses comes down from the mountain with the tablets on which the commandments are written, he finds that in his absence the people have made a golden calf and are worshipping it as their god. He is so angry that he throws the tablets on the ground and shatters them (Ex 32). It is worth noting that the festival held around the golden calf is described at one point as a festival "to honour the LORD". This too epitomises the issue on which the prophets fought. It was not just a simple matter of turning from one god to another: it was the merging of cults, the confusing of idols with the LORD himself.

The prophets of the LORD passionately opposed the worship of the gods of Canaan and the surrounding nations. The chief of these were Baal and his occasionally mentioned female consort Asherah. The title "Baal" was sometimes applied to different gods, so we occasionally find the expression "the Baals". In the early days the struggle was brutal, with a lot of bloodshed, as we see in the Elijah story.

The story presented in the Bible as we now have it is that the LORD had rescued the Israelites from slavery in Egypt and led them into the land he had promised to their ancestors. He had met them at Mount Sinai, given them commandments, and bound them to himself by a covenant. But when they settled into the land they fell into the temptation of worshipping the gods of the land's original inhabitants. This is represented as an apostasy, a falling away from their original faith.

The history is probably rather more complicated. The nation of Israel was always a mixture of races. Archaeological research and close examination of the Bible texts suggests that only a fraction of the Israelites had inherited the memory of being brought out of Egypt. As the nation developed it was their story that gradually prevailed and became the story of the whole nation. It was rather like the way Americans with their mix of national backgrounds and cultures still celebrate a little group of English Puritans as their "Pilgrim Fathers".

Most of those the prophets attacked for worshipping Baal had probably always done so. To them it was not an apostasy, but a refusal to accept the new religion. It was like the situation in Europe when Christianity became established in place of the native paganism. Traditional festivals like Yuletide were given Christian meaning, and churches were built on ancient shrines. The old religion survived, often persecuted under the label of witchcraft, and still survives today both in local traditions and superstitions and in the conscious revival of paganism as a religion. A similar process happened in Israel. Long after the worship of the LORD had become the officially established religion the prophets were still preaching against its corruption by ideas and customs deriving from Baal worship.

The story of the division of the kingdom after the death of Solomon (told, we must realise, from the point of view of the southern kingdom of Judah) says that the king of Israel, Jeroboam, established temples at Bethel and Dan so that people would worship there instead of going to Jerusalem. It was officially still the same God they were worshipping, but the people of Judah came to regard them as idolatrous shrines because of the different imagery used in them. The story as we now have it is strongly coloured by the strict attitudes of later Judaism, with King Jeroboam setting up two golden calves and saying, "People of Israel, here are your gods who brought you out of Egypt" – the very words attributed to Aaron when he set up the notorious Golden Calf shortly after the Exodus (1 Kings 12:25-30; Ex 32:2-4). It is very unlikely that the situation was as "black and white" as that. Bethel and Dan were not new: they were ancient holy places. Elijah and Elisha, who are represented as model prophets of the LORD, lived within that kingdom and seem to have had no problem with these shrines as such.

The prophets' campaigning for the pure worship of the LORD faced opposition from two directions. In the daily life of the ordinary people the old folk religion persisted, while at the level of government there was the infiltration of foreign cults through the alliances and marriages that linked the kings with surrounding nations. This comes to the fore in the reign of Solomon. Although the biblical narrative speaks of him with some pride as a powerful and wise king, and he is honoured as the builder of the temple, he is said to have gone wrong especially in his later years. We are told that he "loved many foreign women", and that among his seven hundred wives and three hundred concubines were many who "led him into the worship of foreign gods". He even built shrines for his wives' gods in the neighbourhood of Jerusalem, including the gods of Moab and Ammon who are described as "disgusting" or "abominations" (1 Kings 11:1-8).

The prophets often describe the worship of other gods in terms of adultery. The nation is pledged in a covenant with the LORD which is a kind of marriage, but the people are flirting with others. Jeremiah says to the people (Jer 2:20-25):

"You are like a wild camel on heat,

running about loose,

rushing into the desert."

"You certainly know how to chase after lovers. Even the worst of women can learn from you."

In representing idolatry in this way some of the prophets display the thoroughly patriarchal and brutal attitude that was part of their culture. Ezekiel in particular treats the theme at great length and seems to revel in sexual images and the degrading of women (see especially Ezek 16 and 23). Some of his images could even be used to justify domestic abuse.

Idolatry is a major theme in the Book of Hosea, a prophet who preached in the northern kingdom between 750 and 725 BC, shortly after Amos's brief visit. Much of the book is a collection of sayings, or poems, on roughly the same theme: the idolatry of the nation, turning from its own God to the gods of the Canaanites (the Baals), mingling with other nations, forming unwise alliances that show distrust of God's protection, and so on. The prayers and sacrifices offered to Baal are compared to a flirtatious wife exchanging gifts with other men while unaware that it is her husband who gives her all the things she needs. At one moment God is angrily vowing to take back all his gifts and strip her naked. At another, he is promising to take her into the desert again and "win her back with words of love", to court her and give her gifts again, so that "she will respond to me there as she did when she was young, when she came from Egypt." (Hos 2:8-15)

This picture of changing emotions reaches a climax near the end of the book (Hos 11:1-9). The image changes from a husband-wife relationship to that of a parent and child. God is saying:

"When Israel was a child, I loved him,

and called him out of Egypt as my son.

But the more I called to him, the more he turned away from me.

My people sacrificed to Baal,

they burnt incense to idols."

Then comes a beautiful, tender description of God's relationship with his beloved child. There is much of the motherly about it:

"Yet I was the one who taught Israel to walk.

I took my people up in my arms,

but they did not acknowledge that I took care of them.

I drew them to me with affection and love,

I picked them up and held them to my cheek;

I bent down to them and fed them."

There follows a threat that because the son has turned away from the parent he will be sent back to Egypt, or taken over by the Assyrians. But then comes a passage that, almost uniquely in the Scriptures, describes God as being torn between anger and tenderness:

"How can I give you up, Israel?

How can I abandon you? ...

My heart will not let me do it!

My love for you is too strong.

I will not punish you in my anger;

I will not destroy Israel again."

Is this a suggestion that God is weakened or brought down to a human level by his softness? Quite the contrary. For Hosea, this tenderness is the supreme expression of divinity:

"For I am God and not man,

I, the Holy One, am with you.

I will not come to you in anger."

In his imagining of the turmoil in the heart of God, fuelled by his own experience of marriage to an unfaithful wife, Hosea raises a question that has haunted religious people down through the ages: the question of the tension between judgment and compassion.

The prophets' uncompromising opposition to religions other than their own is probably one of the least attractive of their features to us today. In this multi-cultural global village the condemnation of other religions as "idolatry" (not to mention "abomination"!) is seen as divisive and harmful. Intolerance and prejudice certainly exist, sometimes in violent forms, but fundamentalist extremes, whether in Islam, Christianity or elsewhere, are deplored by most people whatever their faith. Even the old-fashioned Christian missionary attack on "idol worship" is now generally tempered by the realisation that apparently polytheistic traditions like Hinduism are actually monotheistic at heart:

their "gods" are manifestations of different aspects of the same universal God.

Our modern attitude of tolerance and respect for all religious traditions finds little reflection in the Bible generally and even less in the prophets. One small but perhaps significant exception is in the conversation between the prophet Elisha and the Syrian military commander Naaman. Having been healed of his skin disease through Elisha's help, Naaman tells him that from now on he will not offer sacrifice to any god but the God of Israel. He only asks whether the LORD will pardon him when in the course of his official duty he goes into the temple of the Syrian god Rimmon and bows down. Elisha's answer is not a direct yes or no: he simply says, "Go in peace" (2 Kings 5:18-19). This is virtually the only hint we have in the prophets that some compromise is possible with other religions. The general attitude is complete opposition.

But before we dismiss this battle of religions as irrelevant to the present time, it is worth reflecting on a deeper dimension of it. What made the prophets so angry about this issue?

There was probably an element of nationalism about it, a resentment of the influence of foreign kingdoms and foreign customs. There was also an element of nostalgia that looked back to the nomadic past and its traditions and resented the ways of the settled agricultural and urban community. There was even a sect called the Rechabites who insisted on preserving the old nomadic culture (rather like the Amish in America): they lived in tents, planted no crops, and abstained from wine (Jer 35).

At the same time, there lay beneath the prophets' concern a strong ethical tradition. The Israelite community that traced its origins from the Exodus and the wilderness wanderings had inherited ways that clashed with those of the agricultural and urban community. The indigenous religion of Canaan had a strong emphasis on fertility. Its sexual rituals were anathema in the eyes of those who had inherited the strict code of the desert.

Even human sacrifice was occasionally practised. Drunkenness too would appear disgraceful to a desert culture that knew nothing of vineyards.

In the desert there would have been none of the gross inequality that was a part of the agricultural and urban way of life. A nomadic tribal community does not have the distinction between landlords and tenants. While it might practise trade, it would not have individual merchants becoming wealthy while their neighbours were poor: the community was a tribal one in which everyone benefited from the wealth of the tribal chief. In the desert people are very dependent on each other and need a strict code of behaviour in order to survive. And so it is quite understandable that the clash between the religion inherited from the desert wanderings and the indigenous religion of Canaan should be a matter of basic lifestyle and values. In the minds of the prophets idolatry and injustice were often two sides of the same coin.

With this in mind, we today can perhaps identify with the concerns of the prophets. Their concern for the right religion had a strong association with social justice. While we have moved away from extreme religious intolerance, and would not dream of calling the gods of other nations "abominations", there are still deep spiritual divisions. They are not so much between one religion and another as between different basic perceptions of what life is about. Many of us today are unhappy with the unscrupulous exploitation that is part of global capitalism, the unrestrained competitiveness displayed at all levels of society from the individual to the nation state, and the spiritual emptiness and superficiality of consumerism. If we are sensitive to this, the glamorous images in advertisements and the grand architecture of shopping malls can have the same effect on us as the idolatrous statues and temples had on those Israelite prophets. The clash of cults was a clash of values that had a direct bearing on people's lives. Their language and thought-forms may have been different from ours, but their basic concern was much the same.

7

Facing the End

Under King Josiah of Judah (640-609 BC) there was a determined effort to establish a purer worship of the LORD and root out idolatry. This was sparked off by the discovery (whether genuine or engineered we do not know) of an old book of the Law in the temple. Guided by the advice of a female prophet, Huldah, the king carried out major reforms to the cult (2 Kings 22-23). The nature of those reforms strongly suggests that the book concerned was Deuteronomy, or at least an early version of it. All the local shrines with their idolatrous associations were destroyed, and the temple in Jerusalem designated as the only place where sacrifices could be offered.

The opportunity for these reforms was to some extent provided by a decline in the power of Assyria. It was a period of relative peace and prosperity. Some of the shrines that were destroyed were in the former kingdom of Israel, which suggests that at this time Judah was regaining control over some of the territories that had been taken over by the Assyrians.

But this period of peace and reform was short-lived. Babylon and Egypt were fighting to fill the power vacuum left by Assyria. Josiah tried to intervene to stop an Egyptian army attacking Assyria, and was killed. Babylon gained the supremacy, and within twenty years the kingdom of Judah was no more.

The prophet Zephaniah, who preached during the reign of Josiah, seems to have been inspired by the spirit of reformation but at the same time sharply aware of the looming power of Babylon. His book begins:

"The LORD said, 'I am going to destroy everything on earth, all human beings and animals, birds and fish.'"

But this does not apparently include the kingdom of Judah.

God's purpose there is to cut off all remnants of the worship of Baal and other gods, and to seek out and punish all those who have participated in these practices. Other nations, meanwhile – the Philistines, the Moabites, the Ammonites, the Assyrians and even the faraway Ethiopians – will be utterly destroyed.

Along with this will come a humbling and purification of the survivors. The proud leaders will be removed, leaving behind "a humble and lowly people" who will seek refuge in the God of Israel and live in his ways. And so the book ends on a note of celebration. Israel will be delivered from its humiliation and defeat. God's promise is: "I will make you famous throughout the world and make you prosperous once again". (Zeph 1:2; 3:12-20)

Like most of the prophets, Zephaniah projects his fears and hopes for Israel and surrounding nations onto a cosmic screen. This is part of the style of prophetic hyperbole, a feature that has always been found in poetry. But looking from the point of view of our own time there is perhaps a new relevance in Zephaniah's language. Today there is a real possibility that human greed, conflict and folly will bring about a situation where not only human life but animal life too could be swept off the face of the earth. Or, if that does not happen, there could remain a depleted human race, "a humble and lowly people" to start the hard task of rebuilding civilisation on sounder principles. That rather obscure and grim prophet who lived more than two and a half millennia ago is still able to furnish a "wake up" call to humanity in the twenty-first century.

As the threat of Babylon loomed larger, the outstanding prophet of the time was Jeremiah. His preaching career began in the reign of Josiah and continued until after the destruction of Jerusalem. He was not taken with the other deportees to Babylon, but remained in Judah to the bitter end and eventually, against his will, joined the small group of survivors who migrated to Egypt.

Jeremiah seems to have been somewhat involved in Josiah's

reform of religion. This included, in keeping with the tone of the Book of Deuteronomy, an element of moral earnestness with a stress on loving God with one's whole being. There is a hint that Jeremiah approved of this reformation and was involved in promulgating its principles, but he does not seem to have held out very much hope for it. In his eyes, the people were not ready for a proper reform, and all these efforts would not ultimately prevent the fall of the kingdom (Jer 11:1-8).

In the face of the threat from Babylon, the priests and the professional prophets were doing their "routine" job of reassuring the people that their God would protect them, and that Jerusalem, the Holy City, the dwelling place of God himself, could never come to harm. They were probably able to quote some of the hymns of the temple like:

"There is a river that brings joy to the city of God,

to the sacred house of the Most High.

God is in that city, and it will never be destroyed." (Ps 46:5)

But Jeremiah could see that in view of all its shameless idolatry and injustice Jerusalem was not fit to survive. Like Isaiah and others before him, he denounced the injustice he saw in Jerusalem. On one occasion he stood at the entrance to the temple and challenged the people going in to worship:

"Stop believing these deceitful words, 'We are safe! This is the LORD's Temple, this is the LORD's Temple, this is the LORD's Temple!' Change the way you are living and stop doing the things you are doing. Stop taking advantage of aliens, orphans and widows. Stop killing innocent people in this land. Stop worshipping other gods... You do these things I hate, and then you come and stand in my presence, in my own Temple, and say 'We are safe!' Do you think my Temple is a hiding place for robbers?" (Jer 7:1-17)

He recalled the old temple at Shiloh which had been destroyed centuries before, and foresaw that Jerusalem would suffer the same fate.

Later, he challenged King Josiah's son Jehoiakim with the way he used his power and money on showy extravagant projects that enslaved and impoverished his people:

"Doomed is the man who builds his house by injustice
and enlarges it by dishonesty;
who makes his countrymen work for nothing
and does not pay their wages...
Does it make you a better king
if you build houses of cedar,
finer than those of others?
Your father enjoyed a full life.
He was always just and fair,
and he prospered in everything he did.
He gave the poor a fair trial,
and all went well with him." (Jer 22:13-16)

Throughout this period Jeremiah was the realist. He said of the priests and the "establishment" prophets of his time:

"They act as if my people's wounds were only scratches. 'All is well', they say, when all is not well." (Jer 6:14; 8:11)

"Jeremiah" has become a word for a miserable pessimist, the sort of person who puts a damper on any positive project by saying "it won't work". What is usually forgotten when people use his name in this way is that Jeremiah was actually right. Amid all the self-deceit and false optimism, he was the realist. Even when the Babylonian forces were surrounding Jerusalem, Jeremiah was advising people to go out and surrender to them. In an echo of the Book of Deuteronomy he says:

"Listen! I, the LORD, am giving you a choice between the way that leads to life and the way that leads to death". (Jer 21:8; Deut 30:15)

But there is a stinging irony in the quotation. Whereas in Deuteronomy the way to life was obedience to the commandments and the way to death was disobedience, Jeremiah's message was much more immediate: the "way of life" was to go out and surrender to the Babylonians and the "way of death" was to stay in the city. This message was naturally regarded as treason, and several attempts were made to silence Jeremiah. He was arrested and put on trial several times. On one occasion he was thrown into a dry well and left to die, but King Zedekiah sent men to pull him out, and then he was confined to the court of the palace guard. Zedekiah seems to have had an ambivalent relationship with Jeremiah: he sought advice, but he sought it secretly through fear of how his courtiers and the people generally would react, and in the end he did not take the advice he had asked for (Jer 37-39).

At one point (Jer 29:1-23) Jeremiah wrote a letter to those who had been deported to Babylon, urging them to accept their situation:

"Build houses and settle down. Plant gardens and eat what you grow in them. Marry and have children. Then let your children get married, so that they also may have children. You must increase in numbers and not decrease."

He also urged them to seek the welfare of Babylon and pray for it, because the welfare of that city would be for their good. Once again, he found himself in conflict with those prophets who were holding out false hopes of a quick return. He declared that the exiles would indeed return, but only after a very long time.

After the first fall of Jerusalem, when the Babylonians looted the temple and the royal palace and took away the first batch of deportees, most of the popular prophets were still preaching a message of reassurance, seeing all this as only a temporary setback. But Jeremiah made a yoke of wooden bars and strapped it over his shoulders in order to dramatize his message that Judah and its neighbouring kingdoms must accept the inevitable and submit to the yoke of Babylonian rule. A prophet called Hananiah contradicted him to his face and said that within two years the king, all the exiles and all the temple treasures would be returned to Jerusalem. In the course of their argument, Hananiah made his point by grabbing the yoke from Jeremiah's neck and breaking it. The story then says that Jeremiah did not answer, but went on his way, and that it was some time later that:

"...the LORD told me to go and say to Hananiah, 'The LORD has said that you may be able to break a wooden yoke, but he will replace it with an iron yoke.'" (Jer 27-28)

It is tempting to see this story in the light of a common experience. How often are we lost for words when someone challenges us, and then think of a devastating answer later on! Did Jeremiah decide there was no point in arguing, or was he, being the sensitive person he was, unnerved by Hananiah's invincible confidence? But the explanation is probably more theological. The story is told in this way in order to show that the true prophet only says what God gives him to say: he is totally dependent on God speaking in God's own time.

Having been realistic in prophesying the worst, Jeremiah saw through the disaster to the unchanging faithfulness of God, and was able to say that this was not the end. There are passages that paint a golden picture of the people being back in their own country ruled by a prince of their own and rejoicing in God's blessing (e.g. Jer 30-31). These could well be later additions to the book rather than originating with Jeremiah himself, but there are some that are almost certainly authentic: for example, the little story of how Jeremiah bought a piece of his ancestral property in the conquered territory and buried the deeds in a safe place in the confidence that one day the people of Judah would again have control over their own land (Jer 32:1-15).

Jeremiah's deepest and most far-seeing insight is found in a remarkable passage which sees beyond the return from exile to a whole new relationship of God with his people:

"The LORD says, 'The time is coming when I will make a new covenant with the people of Israel and with the people of Judah... I will put my law within them and write it on their hearts... None of them will have to teach his fellow-countryman to know the LORD, because all will know me, from the least to the greatest...'" (Jer 31:31-34)

Jeremiah saw that having commandments written on stone tablets or in a book was not enough, nor was it enough that people should do the right thing under pressure, responding to the instruction of rulers or priests. The people would only truly be God's people when his ways were written in their hearts so that they were naturally and spontaneously doing his will. This "new covenant" became a central theme in the Christian faith. The expression is used in the account of the Last Supper (Luke 22:20; 1 Cor 11:25), and the very phrase "New Testament" is the Latinised form of what the early Church called "the Scriptures of the New Covenant". Paul describes the essence of Christian experience as being put right with God through faith and knowing a life in which "God has poured out his love into our hearts by means of the Holy Spirit" (Rom 5:1-5).

It is interesting that Jeremiah had already seen that the key to this transformation is forgiveness: "I will forgive their sins and I will no longer remember their wrongs". The story of Jesus in the Gospels emphasises his friendship with sinners and his message of forgiveness. In language that many people use today, the key to a good life is not struggling to obey the rules, but believing that we are unconditionally accepted. To know this is to be set free to love ourselves and others. It seems that in some way Jeremiah had an inkling of this principle six centuries before Christ.

The trauma of the destruction of Jerusalem and the exile to Babylon shows itself in most parts of the Hebrew Scriptures. There is a whole book called "Lamentations". One of the bitterest passages in the Bible is the little Psalm 137, "By the rivers of Babylon we sat down; there we wept when we remembered Zion". It asks the anguished question, "How can we sing a song to the LORD in a foreign land?" And it ends with that terrible cry for vengeance, "Happy are those who pay you back for what you have done to us – who take your babies and smash them against a rock."

The little nation of Judah could well have disappeared as other small nations did, absorbed into the cosmopolitan mixture of the huge Babylonian Empire and the even bigger Persian Empire that succeeded it. Instead, its people have survived to this day and given to the world three of its major faiths.

Among the earlier batch of deportees was the prophet Ezekiel. His book is full of lurid descriptions of the sins of the people and the terrible judgment inflicted on them. At the same time, he presents a positive picture of God's purposes moving forward. His visions in Babylonia showed him that the glory of God that had been in the temple in Jerusalem was now in Babylon, thus answering the question of Psalm 137 as to how a song to the LORD could be sung in a foreign land. With all the predictions of disaster there is a promise that things will one day be restored. Quite early in his book, when he is telling the exiles in Babylon that Jerusalem will be destroyed, he promises that they or their descendants will one day turn back to God and be restored to their land with a new spirit. This is much further developed later in the book, where the promise is that the whole land of Israel will once again be inhabited and cultivated and its cities rebuilt (Ezek 11:14-20; 36:25-26). Echoing Jeremiah's prophecy of a new covenant, he promises that the people will be restored not only materially but spiritually too:

"I will sprinkle clean water on you and make you clean from all your idols and everything else that has defiled you. I will give you a new heart and a new mind. I will take away your stubborn heart of stone and give you an obedient heart." (Ezek 36:25-26)

Ezekiel deals with a problem that was very prominent in the period during and after the Exile. The people had a sense of being punished for the sins of previous generations. This was reinforced by the historical narrative that was probably being compiled at that time. It classifies all the kings as good or bad, mostly bad. A king who was faithful to the LORD and obeyed the commandments brought blessing on himself and the kingdom, but a king who encouraged the worship of other gods and neglected the commandments brought disaster. The historian portrays Josiah, in particular, as an outstandingly godly king, but cannot ignore the fact that he died a violent death at an early age. He explains it by saying that God was still angry about the sins of Josiah's grandfather Manasseh and had determined that the kingdom would be destroyed (2 Kings 23:25-27).

Ezekiel tries to reassure the people that their suffering for the sins of previous generations is not the last word: there is always the opportunity of a new start. He quotes the proverb that was popular among the people at the time: "The parents ate the sour grapes, but the children got the sour taste". This is no longer true, he says: "The person who sins is the one who will die". He then goes into a long exposition of how if a good man's son turns to evil his father's goodness will not avail, but if a wicked man's son turns to good he will be well rewarded and not suffer for his father's sins (Ezek 18).

This points to an important feature of biblical prophecy. In the Ten Commandments, God is represented as one who visits the sins of the fathers on the children to the third and fourth generation (Ex 20:5). We know by experience that people often suffer for the wrongdoing and folly of their ancestors. It happens in family life, as patterns repeat themselves in consecutive generations. It happens also in history: much of the conflict, bitterness and terrorism in the world today is a legacy from oppression inflicted in the past. The tragic situation in Israel and Palestine is the result of decisions made and problems not properly faced a hundred years ago. Fraught relationships between black and white people today have their roots in colonialism and slavery that go back to the eighteenth century or further. It has always been true that the sins of the parents are visited on the children, but we need not interpret Ezekiel as totally denying this fact of life. The essence of biblical prophecy is that it is a message for the time, part of a living dialogue between God and humanity. Ezekiel was not necessarily laying down an eternal principle: he was telling the people what they needed to know at that moment in their history.

One of the best-known passages in Ezekiel is the "dry bones" vision (Ezek 37:1-14). The prophet sees a valley full of dry bones, like the aftermath of a great battle. God asks him whether he thinks these bones can live again, and he replies, "Sovereign LORD, only you can answer that!" He is then commanded to prophesy to the bones, and there is a sound of rattling as all the skeletons come together again – a scene described in the old popular spiritual "Dem Bones". Sinews and flesh and skin appear on them. The prophet then calls upon the four winds of heaven to bring the breath of God into the bodies, and they come to life and stand up. God then interprets the vision to him as a prophecy that the nation of Israel, which now sees itself as dry and dead, will be restored. The people will be brought up from their graves and returned to their own land. This passage is understandably popular among Christians because it is one of the points at which the central New Testament theme of death and resurrection emerges in the Jewish Scriptures.

The last nine chapters of Ezekiel are occupied with a detailed description of the restored temple, the sacrifices to be offered in it, the rebuilt city of Jerusalem and the way in which the land is to be re-occupied by the nation of Israel. This seems to be a kind of blueprint for the future, perhaps intended in part to keep a record of what the city and the land were before the devastation brought about by the Babylonian invasion. There is also a strong element of holiness about it. The temple is to stand alone and not have any other buildings joined to it. There is to be strict separation between the authorised priests of Jerusalem and the other Levites who had taken part in idolatrous worship elsewhere: these are to be simply servants of the temple rather than priests. Foreigners are to be excluded from the temple altogether (see especially Ezek 43:8-9; 44:10-14). Here we see the beginning of the strict and exclusive attitudes that shaped the eventual re-establishment of the Jewish community under Ezra and Nehemiah. This aspiration to a restored and sanctified Jerusalem is summed up in the final words of the book: "And the name of the city from that time on shall be, The LORD is there."

8

New Beginnings

The opening words of Isaiah 40 come like a trumpet call at dawn, a great shout of joy breaking the long silence:

"Comfort, O comfort my people, says your God.

Speak tenderly to Jerusalem, and cry to her that she has served her term, that her penalty is paid, that she has received from the LORD's hand double for all her sins." (Isa 40:1-2, NRSV)

The prophets' promises of better times almost always refer to an uncertain time in the future, something to dream of, but in this passage the good news is about the present moment: something wonderful and significant is happening *now*. God seems to be acknowledging that the people have been punished enough: in fact, the punishment has been twice what they deserved! This is probably a figure of speech expressing the feeling that it is high time the punishment ceased and the people got a taste of God's favour once again. God is speaking here rather like a mother who has over-reacted to her child's naughtiness and now wants to take him in her arms, dry his tears and tell him that she still loves him.

This part of Isaiah (Chapters 40-55) belongs, as we have seen, to a period much later than that of the original prophet. It is a celebration of the new beginning coming to the Jewish people after the destruction of Jerusalem and long years of exile in Babylon. At the same time, this anonymous prophet encourages the people to persevere in faith and offers some very profound reflections on the nature and mission of Israel as the LORD's special people.

There seems to be a kind of "call story" embedded in this opening chapter. The prophet hears God's command telling him to cry out. He asks what he should cry, pointing out that the nation is like grass, like flowers that have withered and faded. He doubts whether there is any positive message to preach in this world where nothing is permanent and human beings are all vulnerable and unreliable. But he receives the answer:

"Yes, grass withers and flowers fade, but the word of our God endures for ever."

Perhaps this prophet had Isaiah in mind, and this was why these words were joined to the Book of Isaiah. Much had changed since Isaiah had promised that God would protect and preserve Jerusalem. The promise seemed to have become a casualty of the change and mortality that is the condition of all human history. But, says the prophet, God's word stands for ever. God never forgets a promise.

For the Jewish exiles in Babylon it was one of those wonderful moments we have occasionally seen in our own time. It was rather like the sudden series of changes in Eastern Europe in 1989, when one totalitarian regime after another was falling and we saw people dancing on the Berlin Wall, or the time when Nelson Mandela was released and the first free elections were held in South Africa. It was to such a moment that the great poet behind Isaiah 40-55 was responding. He was pulling out all the stops and stirring the people up to rejoice. He imagined a great highway being built across the desert from Babylon to Judah, the way for the exiles to return. The description is remarkably suggestive of a modern major road-building project:

"Fill every valley;
level every mountain.
The hills will become a plain,
and the rough country will be made smooth."

He addresses the downcast inhabitants of Jerusalem and says:

"Jerusalem, go up on a high mountain
and proclaim the good news!
Call out with a loud voice, Zion;
announce the good news!
Speak out and do not be afraid.

Tell the towns of Judah

that their God is coming!"

He pictures God coming like a general returning from the battle to share with his people the spoils of victory. But after this warrior image we return to the tenderness with which the passage began, and the image of a shepherd gathering the flock, carrying the lambs in his arms and gently leading the mother sheep.

Just as the first Isaiah had declared that the mighty empire of Assyria was just a tool in the hand of God to chastise his people (Isa 10:5-19), so the second Isaiah sees Cyrus as one called to serve God's purpose of blessing his people:

"Who was it that brought the conqueror from the east,

And makes him triumphant wherever he goes?

Who gives him victory over kings and nations?" (Isa 41:2)

The prophet even sees Cyrus as God's appointed saviour of Israel:

"Thus says the LORD to his anointed, to Cyrus…" (Isa 45:1, NRSV)

The title "God's anointed" that was applied to the kings of Israel now belongs to this foreign emperor! Cyrus himself is of course quite unaware of this. God says to him, "I have given you great honour, although you do not know me". At the same time, the prophet seems to see a possibility that he may become aware of it. God promises him an unstoppable progress, enabling him to subdue nations, depose kings, open doors, break down iron bars, gain access to treasures, all so that "then you will know that I am the LORD, and that the God of Israel has called you by name" (Isa 45:3). An inscription originating from that time talks of the god of Babylon calling Cyrus "by name". This Jewish prophet asserts that it is the God of *Israel* who has done this.

One of the great themes of this part of Isaiah is its constant assertion that the LORD, the God of Israel, is the only God, Lord of the whole world. It is not easy to judge how new this was, as we cannot be sure at what stage the religion of Israel became completely monotheistic. The first of the Ten Commandments was to worship the LORD alone and to have no other gods before him. This did not necessarily imply that no other gods existed. There is a story (1 Sam 4-5) about a battle in which the Israelites took the Ark of the Covenant, the symbol of the presence of the LORD, onto the field and the Philistines captured it. They placed it in the temple of their god Dagon, but the next morning they found Dagon lying on the floor. They set him up again, but on the following morning they found him lying on the floor again and broken in pieces. The assumption behind stories such as this seems to be that other gods do exist, but they are overcome by the greater power of Israel's God.

Some of the prophets saw in world events the hand of the LORD who ruled the entire world. The original Isaiah had described Assyria as being only a tool the LORD was using to chastise his own people: having used it he would discard it. But this second part of Isaiah presses the message home with even more force. He encourages people not to look at the great temples of Babylon but at the whole world over which the LORD reigns:

"To the LORD the nations are nothing,

no more than a drop of water;

the distant islands are as light as dust." (Isa 40:15)

The prophet reiterates sayings like:

"Besides me there is no other;

there never was and never will be."

"I am the first, the last, the only God;

there is no other god but me." (Isa 43:10; 44:6; see also 41:4; 45:5 etc.)

The word "other" is provided by the translators. The prophet seems to have positively revelled in the statement: "there is no god"! He was challenging the Jewish exiles to look the impressive "gods" of Babylon in the face and say, "I don't believe in you – you don't exist!" There is a kind of liberating atheism about these statements. All the gods and powers of the world are stripped of their divinity, and there is nothing to which people need to be in thrall.

This was a necessary assertion if the Jews were going to maintain their faith in the face of Babylon's temples and statues that were so much more impressive than anything in Jerusalem. It was easy to feel that the powerful gods of Babylon had defeated the God of Israel. In face of this the prophet constantly asserts that the LORD is not just the God of Israel but the one and only God of the whole world.

He delights in making fun of the "gods" of Babylon. He talks sarcastically of the makers of idols choosing a wood that "will not rot" and making sure the image is properly set up so that it "won't fall down", checking that the soldering is good and fastening it with nails so that it cannot be moved – inviting the obvious question: what is the use of a god who cannot move? Even the humblest of *real* living creatures can move! (Isa 40:20; 41:7, NRSV)

He gives a satirical account of the making of a "god". The carpenter chooses a suitable tree in the forest and waits for it to grow. When he has cut it down he uses part of it for fuel. He bakes bread with it and cooks meat with it. He sits in front of the fire and says, "How nice and warm!" Then he shapes the rest of it into an image, bows down to it and says, "You are my god – save me!" He has forgotten that he himself has made this "god"! But the real God of Israel says to his people, "I created you". (Isa 44:9-21)

Another satirical picture is of the flight of the defeated people from Babylon, carrying their gods to safety "loaded on donkeys, a burden for the backs of tired animals". The prophet then draws the contrast with the LORD saying to his people: "I made you and will care for you; I will give you help and rescue you" (Isa 46:1-4). This conjures up an image of two kinds of religion that are still with us today. There is a religion that holds people down, making them suppress their doubts and obey the rules, demanding intellectual effort to defend it, urging them to hectic activity and engendering a constant feeling of guilt and fear. This truly is "a burden for the backs of tired animals". In contrast to this is the kind of faith that is experienced as a sense of being supported rather than a faith we ourselves have to support.

But alongside this grand vision of the one and only God of all time and space, this prophet still talks of a God who has an intimate relationship with the little nation of Israel:

"Israel, the LORD who created you says,

'Do not be afraid – I will save you.

I have called you by name – you are mine...

I will give up whole nations to save your life,

because you are precious to me..." (Isa 43:1-5)

The prophet sees the universal lordship of God as primarily acting on behalf of one people, Israel. On the other hand, it is clear that in this book the idea of Israel as God's chosen people is not a merely triumphalist one: it is tied up with a witnessing and redemptive mission to the world, even involving suffering.

This paradox perhaps says something about the mystery of God. The God who is in and through all things is at the same time in every particular thing in a particular way. In the Bible, God's love is not a universal abstract principle, but something much more intimate and special. We might express it by saying that God cares for everybody, but that he cares for each individual as if they were the only one.

At one point the prophet challenges the "gods" of Babylon to "do something good or bring disaster; fill us with fear and awe! You and all you do are nothing..." (Isa 41:23-24). These words were no doubt meant for the Jews who might still have some residual fear of these gods. The prophet is pointing out that there is nothing to fear. These gods are non-existent: they can do no good and no harm.

But this raises a fundamental question, one that could be a chink in the prophet's armour. What about the God of Israel? Where is the evidence that *he* actually does anything? After all, the people who believed they were under his special protection have seen their city and their temple destroyed, and are living under the rule of people who worship other gods. The prophet is calling people away from belief in all these impressive gods with their great temples and richly adorned images, but calling them to what? To a God who has no image at all and cannot be seen!

This perception of God is fundamental to the biblical faith. The God who cannot be represented by any visible or tangible image is the real God, the one whose hidden power overcomes all the visible powers of the world. As the New Testament Letter to the Hebrews puts it: "To have faith is to be sure of the things we hope for, to be certain of the things we cannot see" (Heb 11:1)·

To return to the history: the return from exile was a dream come true, but like all dreams come true it was not perfect. Visionaries can see the great sweep of history, but the details are more complex and down to earth. Like the "rainbow nation" that emerged from the end of apartheid in South Africa, like the long-awaited reunification of Germany, and like the election of the first black President of the United States, the long-term reality never quite lives up to that first moment of euphoria. The prophets of the decades that followed the return to Jerusalem were dealing with yet another new situation, with its problems as well as its hopes.

The process of resettlement and rebuilding did not go smoothly. There is evidence of a tension between the returned exiles and the people already in the land. Some of these were probably descended from Jews who had not been taken into exile. Others were perhaps immigrant or deportees who had come to live there in the meantime. A cultural gap had probably opened up during the half century of exile. The current inhabitants of Judah regarded the returned exiles as unwanted immigrants, while the exiles saw themselves as maintaining the pure worship of the LORD against the degenerate practices of the "people of the land".

The prophet Haggai was preoccupied with the rebuilding of the temple. His sayings are all contained within one year, the second year of Darius king of Persia, i.e. about 521 BC. By this time the site of the temple had been cleared and foundations laid for a new one, but the work had been left off, partly because of opposition from other inhabitants of the country. Haggai was concerned that while people were enriching themselves and building fine houses there was no real effort to start rebuilding the temple. He saw the poor harvests brought about by drought and blight as a sign of God's disapproval, and appealed to Zerubbabel the governor and Joshua the high priest to organise a new start on the work. While people lamented that this new temple seemed a very poor thing compared with the old one, Haggai promised that God would "shake heaven and earth, land and sea" and "overthrow all the nations", so that their wealth would flow into Jerusalem and "the new temple will be more splendid than the old one" (Hagg 2:3-9).

This book has none of the passion for justice that characterises most of the other prophets' books. Its priorities are all around the temple and formalised religious practice. At the same time, this comparatively modest dream did come true. The new temple was completed soon afterwards and stood for nearly five hundred years until King Herod replaced it with a much grander one in 20-18 BC.

Zechariah is said to have preached "in the second year of Darius", which means he was an exact contemporary of Haggai. It was a time of peace in most of the surrounding countries, no doubt because of the strong rule of the Persian Empire, but Jerusalem was still languishing in a poor and depressed state, with the temple not yet rebuilt. Zechariah's message is much the same as that of Haggai – the promise of a new age of prosperity for Jerusalem with the rebuilding of the temple – but it is expressed much more dramatically with strange visions and symbols. He sees a vision of Joshua the high priest in filthy clothes, representing not only poverty but also a sense of the cumulative guilt of the people. Satan is standing by him, accusing him. The figure of Satan in the Hebrew Scriptures is not the dark, completely evil force with which we associate the name today. He is called "the Satan", which means "the accuser". As in the Book of Job, he seems to be the one whose function is to cast suspicion on those who serve God: a kind of "devil's advocate". In Zechariah's vision, the angel of the LORD rebukes the Satan and decrees that Joshua should be dressed in fine, festive clothes. He promises that if he continues to walk in God's ways he will have charge of God's house, and the guilt of the people will be taken away. Zerubbabel, the governor, also receives praise and encouragement. Having laid the foundations of the new temple, he is promised that he will complete the building of it (Zech 3; 4:8-10).

In contrast to the exact dating of Haggai and Zechariah, the Book of Malachi is very difficult to place. Its title gives no indication of Malachi's ancestry or home town, as is the case with other prophets. In fact, it is suggested that it is not the name of a prophet at all, but simply a title meaning "my messenger", picked up from the first verse of the third chapter:

"The LORD Almighty answers, 'I will send my messenger to prepare the way for me...'"

The main concern of the book is the low standard of sacrifices offered in the new temple, and a warning that when the long-awaited presence of the LORD comes to the temple it will be to judge and purify it (Mal 3:1-4).

A rather different vision is found in the last part of the Book of Isaiah (chapters 56-66), which is roughly contemporary with Haggai and Zechariah. It is a glorious mixture of ethical challenge, agonised prayer and visions of the future. The situation after the return of the exiles was evidently complex and messy. A good part of this prophet's preaching is occupied with the faults of the people. He rebukes the leaders for their laziness and complacency while the people are being attacked and persecuted (Isa 56:9-12). Some of those who had never left the land were still worshipping other gods, some even practising child sacrifice (Isa 57:5). The land was open to exploitation because no strong defences had yet been established, and the returned exiles who had kept the faith and traditions alive throughout their time in Babylon now saw themselves as the true people of God under persecution.

The prophet sees God "displeased" by it all and "appalled" that there is no one else to intervene, and so deciding to enter the fray himself and come clothed in righteousness and salvation, vengeance and fury (Isa 59:15-20). This is the prelude to a passage (Isa 60) describing a complete transformation of the situation. It begins with words that are familiar from Christmas carol services:

"Arise, Jerusalem, and shine like the sun;

the glory of the LORD is shining on you!"

But this is not a promise for the whole world. It is for Israel and for Jerusalem in particular, as is shown by the next words:

"Other nations will be covered by darkness,

but on you the light of the LORD will shine;

the brightness of his presence will be with you.

Nations will be drawn to your light,

and kings to the dawning of your new day."

The other nations of the world will willingly bring their tributes to be presented in the temple:

"The wealth of the nations will be brought to you;

from across the sea their riches will come."

Not only will animals from Judean pastures be sacrificed in the temple, but "all the sheep of Kedar and Nebaioth", and God will accept them all.

The return of the exiles from all the places to which they have been scattered is likened to homing pigeons flocking to their roost. The gates of the city will be open day and night, as in the New Testament vision of the New Jerusalem (Rev 21:25-26), to receive the constant procession of people bringing tribute. The city will be more glorious than ever:

"I will bring you gold instead of bronze,

silver and bronze instead of iron and wood,

and iron instead of stone."

This period after the Babylonian exile raises the question: what kind of new beginning was this to be? As we have seen, Ezekiel had his own vision of it as a restoration of the holiness of Jerusalem. This was followed up by the very practical concerns of Haggai and Zechariah, and later by the work of Ezra in re-constituting the community under the Torah and so becoming virtually the founder of Judaism as a religion. The Book of Nehemiah tells of a day on which Ezra read the whole Torah to a great assembly of the people in a public square. The people then confessed their sins and solemnly renewed their covenant to obey God's laws (Neh 8-9). Particular emphasis was laid on laws of exclusion. There was a firm determination that the LORD's people should never again lapse into the idolatry that had brought about their conquest and exile. The Jewish people and their religious practice must be kept pure. All foreigners were to be excluded from the worshipping community, and intermarriage between Jews and Gentiles was forbidden (Neh 13:1-3; Ezra 9-10).

This was a blow to some of the returned exiles. Many Jews had probably served in the courts of the Babylonian emperors and nobility, and for that purpose they had been made eunuchs. This has been normal practice in many cultures: it ensures the safety of the women in the harem, and it avoids any succession disputes if a servant in the royal household should happen to father a child by a queen or princess. The humiliation of castration and the consequent inability to have children must have been very keenly felt by men in the Jewish tradition with its special emphasis on the continuity of the people of God and the idea that we live on through our children. It was even more reinforced by the stipulation in the Law that no-one damaged in the genitals could be admitted to "the assembly of the LORD" (Deut 23:1). By this time the first five books of the Bible (the Torah) had most probably reached the form in which we now have them, and the Jewish community was being solemnly re-constituted under this Torah. Ezra and others took its commandments very seriously, which would certainly mean that eunuchs were excluded from the most sacred parts of the Temple and the cult.

They were also very concerned about the purity of the race. Ezra and Nehemiah took extreme measures against those who had married outside the Jewish community (Ezra 9; Neh 13:23-28). Genealogies at that time became more important than ever: the Torah decreed that non-Jewish people, especially those of certain neighbouring nations, should be excluded from the congregation "to the tenth generation" (Deut 23:3). The little Book of Ruth, with its story of the kind Moabite woman who remained faithful to her Jewish mother-in-law, married into a Jewish family, and became the great-grandmother of King David, was probably written around this time in opposition to these exclusive tendencies.

The prophet of Isaiah 56-66, while, as we have seen, still adhering to the idea of the Jewish nation being restored to a position of superiority, saw somewhat further than Ezra and his like. He says (Isa 56:1-8):

"For thus says the LORD:
to the eunuchs who keep my sabbaths,
who choose the things that please me
and hold fast my covenant,
I will give, in my house and within my walls,
a monument and a name
better than sons and daughters..."

A similar promise is given to the foreigners who "join

themselves to the LORD" and keep his commandments. One result of the Exile was probably a wider spreading of Jewish beliefs that meant there were some people who were not Jews by race but who identified themselves with the Jewish religion. The prophet asserts that the LORD will joyfully welcome these people in his temple and accept their offerings:

"...for my house shall be called a house of prayer
for all peoples."

This message of wide inclusion did not prove popular in Judaism in the centuries that followed. Provision was eventually made for Gentiles to convert to Judaism through circumcision and other rituals, but men who were not circumcised, as well as those whose genitals were incomplete, continued to be strictly barred.

The New Testament (Acts 8:26-40) gives us the moving story of an Ethiopian eunuch returning from Jerusalem where he had gone to worship although he could never truly be part of the holy community. The Christian evangelist Philip meets him and tells him the story of Jesus. Eventually they come across a watering place, and the eunuch asks, "What is to keep me from being baptised?" He has realised that he can be fully accepted and baptised into the new community of God's people. Before Philip approached him he was reading from the scroll of Isaiah the words about the one who was "despised and rejected of men" (Isa 53). If he continued to read on afterwards he would have very soon come to this passage about God welcoming both eunuchs and foreigners into his house of prayer. This anonymous prophet of the last chapters of Isaiah foreshadowed the radical inclusiveness of the Christian message.

9

Prophecy and Prediction

The most popular understanding of the word "prophet" is that it is someone who predicts the future, but when we look at the biblical prophets, we have to be careful what we mean by this.

There is certainly a strong element of prediction in the role of a prophet. In early times another word for a prophet was "seer". This is featured in the story of the first encounter between Samuel and the future king Saul (1 Sam 9-10). Saul is sent by his father, a wealthy farmer called Kish, to look for his donkeys that have gone astray. After he and his servant have wandered over a wide area without success, the servant suggests they return home, because by now Saul's father will be more worried about them than about the donkeys. Then Saul remembers that in a nearby town there is a "man of God" who is held in high honour and whose words always come true. They decide to visit this man, first making sure that they have a quarter shekel of silver to pay him. The narrator points out that what is now called a "prophet" used to be called a "seer". As Saul and the servant make their way towards the town, they make enquiries and are informed that the seer is just on his way to the shrine to bless a sacrifice in preparation for a feast.

The narrator now reveals that the man is Samuel, the recognised leader of the nation, whom the people have petitioned to establish a monarchy. On the previous day Samuel has received a message from God telling him that the man who is going to visit him has been chosen to be the king. Samuel immediately assures Saul that the donkeys have been found. He then invites Saul and the servant to join in the feast and stay the night. The next morning he escorts them out of the town, but sends the servant ahead a little way so that he can have a private word with

Saul. He then takes a phial of oil, pours it on Saul's head, kisses him, and tells him he is anointed to be king of Israel.

He then sends him on his way, giving him three predictions about the journey. First, he will meet some men who will confirm that the donkeys have been found. Then he will meet some people who will give him food. Then he will meet a group of ecstatic prophets playing musical instruments, dancing and shouting, and he will be taken up into their ecstasy and join them. Each of these predictions comes true.

Prediction is very common in the Bible stories. There are many stories of God appearing to people or speaking to them to tell them what will happen, and of prophets making predictions to individuals about imminent events. In fact prediction is such a common motif in the Bible stories that we tend hardly to notice it. These predictions are not confined to the early prophets we might think of as "primitive". Isaiah predicts the collapse of the kingdoms of Israel and Syria under attack from the Assyrians (Isa 7:13-16). Jeremiah predicts that his opponent Hananiah will be dead within the year (Jer 28:16-17).

We cannot prove, of course, that these predictions and their fulfilments literally happened. Some are fairly obviously fictional, such as the detailed outline of the future history of Israel given to Abraham (Gen 15:13-14). Some of the incidents in the lives of the prophets of around Elijah's time sound like legends. A prediction made by Amos is contradicted by the history: he said that King Jeroboam would die in battle because of his sins, but the historical narrative of the kings of Israel seems to imply that he died a natural death (Amos 7:11; see 2 Kings 14:29). The predictions of the fall of Babylon and its king in the Book of Isaiah (e.g. Isa 14:3-23; 46:1-2) seem not to have come true. Babylon was taken over by Cyrus but remained as the capital of the Persian Empire: there was no catastrophic collapse. On other predictions, such as Jeremiah's prophecy that the exiles would be in Babylon for seventy years (Jer 29:10), it is more difficult to judge. A point in favour of this one is its inaccuracy: the exiles actually began to return after about fifty years, which suggests that Jeremiah quite rightly thought it would be a long time but had the faith to believe it would happen.

At their most believable, the great biblical prophets foresaw the future because they had a deep insight into the way things were going in the present. This was not only political insight but faith: the conviction that a wrong way of living would have consequences, and that right living and trusting in God was the best security. They understood their message not as predicting the remote future but as the message God had for the nation at that moment. The real value of their preaching, and the reason why it was remembered and recorded, was not the accuracy of their predictions but the power and continuing relevance of their message.

Usually, when the great preaching prophets talked of the future, they were not making the kind of predictions made by fortune-tellers, astrologers or Old Moore's Almanac. They were not stating that things would definitely happen because it was "in the stars" or decreed by "fate". Their prophecies were warnings, wake-up calls to bring the people to their senses. A simple example of this is in the story of Jonah. Jonah prophesied that the city of Nineveh would be destroyed within forty days because of its wickedness, but when the people repented God "changed his mind" and did not destroy it (Jonah 3:10). Unlike Jonah, most of the prophets balanced their dire predictions with appeals to the people to change their ways and so avoid the catastrophe that would come if they continued as they were (e.g. Jer 7:7).

As we have seen, the issue of true and false prophecy was a particularly sharp one for Jeremiah. He seems to have developed a rough rule for distinguishing between true and false prophets, a rule that was at least true in the time in which he lived. The true prophets, he said, had bad news. As for those who preached good news, only time would tell whether they were speaking the truth (Jer 28:8-9).

The idea that the main function of the prophets was to make predictions about events far into the future has been a feature of Christian tradition from the beginning. The early Christians, in their declaration that Jesus was the expected Messiah, searched the Jewish Scriptures for evidence to back it up. This is well illustrated in the story of Jesus, after the resurrection, talking with two of his disciples on the road to Emmaus, when he "explained to them what was said about himself in all the Scriptures, beginning with the books of Moses and the writings of all the prophets" (Luke 24:27). Paul, apparently repeating an already current Christian "creed", says:

"I passed on to you what I received, which is of the greatest importance: that Christ died for our sins, as written in the Scriptures; that he was buried and that he was raised to life three days later, as written in the Scriptures... (1 Cor 15:3-4)

This led to the general assumption among Christians that the main, if not the only, function of these Scriptures, was to point forward to Jesus. The "proof" of the Christian message was seen by the early Christians, and is still seen by many, in the way Jesus fulfilled the predictions of Scripture.

However, it is clear that this was not how the original prophets themselves saw it. Take for instance the famous words of Isaiah about the virgin who would bear a child and call him Immanuel (Isa 7:13-16). When we read them in context from the beginning of the chapter we can see that they were uttered in a specific situation. Isaiah was speaking to Ahaz, the king of Judah. The neighbouring kingdoms of Israel and Syria had formed an alliance to make war against the Assyrians, and were putting strong pressure on Judah to join them. They were threatening to invade Judah and replace Ahaz with a king more amenable to their plans. The people of Judah were in a state of panic, trembling "like trees shaking in the wind". Isaiah was urging

Ahaz not to be drawn into any foolish strategy but to keep calm and trust God. He spoke contemptuously of these "powers", saying that they are "no more dangerous than the smoke from two smouldering sticks".

In order to reinforce his point Isaiah makes a specific prediction. A young woman is pregnant, and her son will be called Immanuel, which means "God is with us". It is not stated who this young woman is: it could be Isaiah's wife, or a member of the royal family. The prediction is that by the time this child is able to choose between good and bad – probably in the sense of taking or refusing food – the whole situation will have been transformed, and the threat from the kings of Syria and Israel will be no more.

Isaiah's words in this situation have become familiar from Christmas carol services and Handel's *Messiah*. To quote from the Authorised Version:

"Behold, a virgin shall conceive, and bear a son, and shall call his name Immanuel."

Matthew's Gospel takes this as a prediction that Jesus would be born of a virgin (Matt 1:22-23). This is based partly on an ambiguity in the meaning of a word. The Hebrew word generally means a young woman, but the word used in the Greek translation, the one most familiar to the early Christians, specifically means "virgin".

However, when we read the words in their original context we see that they had a particular meaning at the time. If Isaiah had been simply predicting something about a child to be born seven hundred years later, no one would have understood what he was talking about and it would not have given any comfort or presented any challenge to his hearers. It would not have been remembered and written down, and so would not have got into the Bible at all.

Many of the so-called "prophecies of Christ" are not so much predictions as *aspirations*. When Isaiah talked of the new David who would be a good and righteous king and bring universal peace (Isa 11:1-9), he most probably understood himself not as a soothsayer predicting something but as a dreamer expressing the deepest longings of the people. There had been so many corrupt, unjust, disappointing kings, and the prophet was putting into words the longing of the people for a new and better David.

Does this mean that we are wrong to associate the words of the prophets with the story of Jesus, as Christians have done for practically two thousand years? Certainly not. These prophecies are expressions of faith in a God who cares for his people and will not leave them oppressed and deprived forever. That is the kind of God Jews believe in, and this belief is what has kept the Jewish faith alive. For Christians this faith is grounded in what they see of the character of God through Jesus. Isaiah did not know about the birth of Jesus that happened seven hundred years after his time, but what makes his words relevant and inspiring to us is his faith in the future. He believed better times would come because "God is with us". Christians quite rightly see in this a foreshadowing of the coming of Jesus into the world, because Jesus is a sign that God is with us in an even closer and deeper way than Isaiah imagined.

Similarly, when Christians read Isaiah's dream of the ideal king they see Jesus as the ultimate answer to those centuries of longing: not literally as a political leader, but as the inaugurator of a kingdom based on values and methods radically different from the conventional concept of power, a kingdom that is not like the kingdoms of this world. We are quite right to see the connection, so long as we do not make the historical mistake of thinking that this is what the words meant at the time Isaiah said them.

To read the Old Testament *simply* as a Christian book is rather insensitive to the fact that it was the Jewish community that produced these writings, and many generations of Jews have found rich inspiration in them without ever associating them with Jesus. It also cuts us off from the living experience of the original writers and preachers who had their own immediate concerns. Isaiah was not sitting down to write predictions of someone who would come into the world seven hundred years later. He had a message for that moment. But at the same time the poetic richness of his words and the authentic faith that shone through them meant that people down through the generations could see new and deeper meaning in them, culminating for Christians in the life, death and resurrection of Jesus.

Ironically, while we would not know about the prophets if they were not in the Bible, the fact of their being in the Bible tends to cut them off from us as people and dampen the power of their original message. When a piece of writing becomes "Holy Scripture" there is a subtle change in the way we read it and the meaning we give to it. We become blind to its creative, poetic power and start treating it as supernaturally revealed *information*. We fit it into our framework of beliefs and interpret it in a way that will not contradict anything else we believe. We do not so much *read* it as *revere* it. Many Bibles still today are printed in a style that we rarely use for any other book: thin, gold-edged pages, double columns, and every sentence numbered. This format hides the difference between poetry and prose and flattens out all the variety and vibrant life in the words. It is then read in short extracts, from a brass lectern in a solemn voice, followed by the words "This is the word of the Lord" to which the congregation makes the automatic response, "Thanks be to God". Nothing could be further from the context in which the words of the prophets were originally said or the experience of those who heard them for the first time.

It has been said that modern human beings have acquired a new sense – the sense of historical relativity. We live in an age of rapid change, so that we are all aware from quite a young age that the world is different for every generation. We all know what it is to look at an old photograph in disbelief: did they really wear hats like *that*? The older ones among us have seen enormous changes within our own lifetime. The food we eat, our social customs and etiquette, even our beliefs and moral standards, are not the same as when we were young, and even more different from the world of our parents and grandparents. This means that when we read something that was written in a previous era, even within living memory, we know that we must make some allowance for the difference between the writer's culture and our own.

Because of this we are not content, as previous generations were, to read the Bible as if it had been written yesterday as a message directly to us. We want to know who the original writers were, what their situation was, and what they were really trying to say. This is good: it can give us a multi-dimensional view of the prophets. We see them as real people in real life situations, and at the same time we can see beyond them to the timeless significance of their words. We can begin to understand something of what prompted them to speak and the passions that moved them. We can appreciate too the motivation of those who followed them, all those people who remembered their sayings, recorded, amplified and adapted them down through the generations. We have an inkling of their original meaning, but at the same time we can see the new meanings they acquired in different generations and the meaning they have for Christians in the light of Jesus. We can then, quite justifiably and in keeping with that long tradition, re-interpret them again as we see their relevance for our own time. This is much more interesting and relevant than simple fulfilment of predictions.

There is one prophet for whom the question of true prediction has a particular significance: the prophet behind the second part of Isaiah. For him it is a recurring theme. He pictures the LORD calling the nations together and challenging them:

"Which of their gods can predict the future?
Which of them foretold what is happening now?" (Isa 43:9)

"Do not be afraid, my people!

You know that from ancient times until now

I have predicted all that would happen,

and you are my witnesses." (Isa 44:8)

The God of Israel makes fools of the Babylonian fortune-tellers and frustrates the predictions of their astrologers:

"But when my servant makes a prediction,

when I send a messenger to reveal my plans,

I make those plans and predictions come true." (Isa 44:26)

For this prophet, this ability to foretell the future is a proof that the God of Israel is the true God:

"Remember what happened long ago;

acknowledge that I alone am God

and that there is no one else like me.

From the beginning I predicted the outcome;

long ago I foretold what would happen ..." (Isa 46:9-10)

It may be that the prophet here is recalling the reassuring words of the original Isaiah almost two hundred years before, that God would care for Jerusalem and restore its glory, and now he sees these predictions coming true in the imminent return of the Jews from exile and the rebuilding of Jerusalem.

But this question of the fulfilment of prophecy as a proof of God is a difficult one for us today. The New Testament writers set great store by it. For them the Hebrew Scriptures were packed with prophecies that proved that Jesus was the Messiah. The first two chapters of Matthew's Gospel repeatedly point out how Scripture was fulfilled in the birth and infancy of Jesus. Prophecies are quoted about the virgin birth, Bethlehem as the birthplace, the time spent in Egypt, the slaughter of the children of Bethlehem, and the residence in Nazareth. All the Gospels link details of the story of Jesus with Old Testament prophecies, especially in their accounts of his suffering and death.

We today, with our scientific and critical minds, are not convinced about all of these. Some of the "proofs" look a bit contrived, based on an interpretation of the scriptural passages that violates their original meaning. In spite of what Mathew says, there is no statement in the Hebrew Scriptures that says the Messiah will live in Nazareth. Similarly, the quotation from Hosea, "I called my Son out of Egypt" (Matt 2:15; Hos 11:1) originally had a different meaning altogether. The "son" referred to is the nation of Israel, which God called out of slavery in Egypt.

The argument from prophecy also raises the difficult question: how do we know these "predictions" were fulfilled? It seems very naïve to say that things prophesied centuries before were fulfilled in detail, and therefore Jesus must be who Christians claim he is. All we know is that certain things were written centuries before the time of Jesus, and that some people writing just after the time of Jesus *said* that these things happened to him. The stories could have been made up in the light of the "predictions". This is not proof in any sense that we recognise today.

Nevertheless some people are firmly convinced of the reality of prophecy. They search the Bible for anything that might refer specifically to things happening in the world today, particularly in the Middle East, and confidently proclaim that the return of Christ and the end of the world are going to happen in a very short time. Some have even named dates, resulting in great embarrassment accompanied by unconvincing re-interpretations when those dates pass and nothing happens. With all this in mind, what are we to make of the second Isaiah's claim that God shows himself to be God by predicting what is to happen and then bringing it about? It is hard to prove that this is so, and many have made fools of themselves by trying. Is there any point in these assertions that prophecies made many years before have been fulfilled?

Perhaps there is, if we look not at the details but at the broad sweep of history. There are some facts that are quite impressive. The Hebrew Scriptures come to us from a very small community: the little kingdom of Israel that even in its heyday was never a major power, the even smaller kingdom of Judah that was hardly more than one walled city and a few smaller towns, the community of exiles living as a minority in the great city of Babylon, and the even smaller community that returned to rebuild Jerusalem. The claims this little nation made, that one day its God would teach the whole world his ways and that their king would reign to the ends of the earth (Isa 2:4; Ps 72:8-11) must have seemed extremely unlikely at the time. One wonders how seriously they were taken even by those who made them: were they expressing wild aspirations, or were they just following the conventions of court poetry? And yet in strange ways they have come true. People all over the world today live by the teachings that originated in that little kingdom, and monarchs, presidents and prime ministers of some of the most powerful nations in the world go to church and bow in worship to the one who was called "King of the Jews".

Is this fulfilment of prophecy a proof of the existence of God, or is it testimony to the power of dreams and poetry to change the world? Are prophecies self-fulfilling? In the words of Alexander Pope, "hope springs eternal in the human breast". Is it this hope in itself that slowly but inevitably transforms the world? Believers say it is God, but why should it not be both? Was it a slip of the tongue, or a profound insight, when a New Testament writer (1 John 5:4, NRSV) said, without even mentioning God, "And this is the victory that conquers the world, our faith"? And is there more meaning than we realise in the words Jesus sometimes said after a miracle of healing (e.g. Mark 5:34; Luke 7:50; 17:19; 18:42): "Your faith has made you well" or "Your faith has saved you"?

Whatever the answer, the message of the Second Isaiah is a challenge to put one's trust in a God who is invisible, intangible and cannot be pinned down, and yet becomes real to those who turn away from the illusory certainties of the world's religions and ideologies and live by faith in the unseen. Living by faith in this way can open our eyes to patterns in history and in human life that make sense and sustain hope.

10

Dreams Can Change the World

The Book of Isaiah begins with the words "The vision of Isaiah...". This is essentially what the biblical prophets were: visionaries, dreamers. The words "I have a dream" are now forever associated in our minds with Dr Martin Luther King. He too was a preacher, a Baptist pastor steeped in the language of the Bible, but no one could accuse him of preaching dull religious platitudes. His reading of the Bible inspired the dream of real change in the world of here and now. That dream led him straight into political engagement and ultimately cost him his life. Today, fifty years on, we can already see signs of his dream coming true. The injustice and inequality against which he and his friends battled are still with us and erupt in unrest from time to time: fifty years, after all, is a short time in the long history of the world. But there has been enough change in that time to show us that dreams do indeed have the power to make a difference.

As with all great poets, the prophets' dreams were sometimes nightmares. Isaiah, the singer of the vineyard song, sees a land polluted and depleted, a people who have lost all joy in living (Isa 24). As we read it we can surely see it reflecting the fears of our own time:

"The earth dries up and withers; the whole world grows weak; both earth and sky decay... Fewer and fewer remain alive. The grapevines wither, and wine is becoming scarce... In the city everything is in chaos, and people lock themselves in their houses for safety... This is what will happen in every nation all over the world. It will be like the end of harvest, when the olives have been beaten off every tree and the last grapes picked from the vines."

Depletion of resources, huge loss of life through war, famine and climate change, and the resultant breakdown of civilised society – how like the nightmares that haunt today's world! Isaiah spells out the reason:

"The earth lies polluted

under its inhabitants;

for they have transgressed laws,

violated the statutes,

broken the everlasting covenant."

This is not quite the language we would use, but we can recognise the underlying principle. The problem is not just one of technology: it is deeper than that. Human beings in their greed and carelessness have polluted the earth by working against nature rather than with it and ignoring the harmonious relationship – the "covenant" – that humanity should have with its environment.

Though the effects of this are inevitably felt more by the poor, we are seeing today that the rich countries will not escape them in the long run. Extreme weather conditions, social unrest, massive migration and war over resources will affect us all. In the light of this even the ups and downs of our domestic economy that usually dominate our politics become secondary. Isaiah sees this too:

"Everyone will meet the same fate – the priests and the people, slaves and masters, buyers and sellers, lenders and borrowers, rich and poor."

We are indeed "all in it together".

Jeremiah had a nightmare that is perhaps even more chilling. It seemed to him like the undoing of creation itself (Jer 4:23-26):

"I looked at the earth – it was a barren waste;

at the sky – there was no light.

I looked at the mountains – they were shaking,

and the hills were rocking to and fro.

I saw that there were no people;

even the birds had flown away.
The fertile land had become a desert;
its cities were in ruins."

In reading this we can almost feel that he was foreseeing a modern nuclear war or an environmental disaster. It is only when he concludes the sentence with "... because of the LORD's fierce anger" that we begin to feel he is not speaking our language. Can we really believe in the kind of God who would destroy the world in a fit of anger? This brings home to us the fact that the preaching of the prophets is in some ways alien, coming to us from a very different culture. At the same time it can challenge us to reflection. Who are we to scorn the religious ideas of another culture when we ourselves have created a world in which all these things could quite easily happen? Perhaps it is no longer the anger of God but our own anger we need to be afraid of.

But, like many protesters, the prophets had glorious positive visions too:
"they shall beat their swords into ploughshares,
and their spears into pruning-hooks;
nation shall not lift up sword against nation,
neither shall they learn war any more." (Isa 2:4, NRSV)
"The desert will rejoice,
and flowers will bloom in the wilderness.
The desert will sing and shout for joy...
The blind will be able to see,
and the deaf will hear.
The lame will leap and dance,
and those who cannot speak will shout for joy." (Isa 35:1-6)

If Isaiah saw it, we today have even more reason to see that when things are right with humanity there is no limit to how the world can be transformed. We may be appalled by the injustice and unnecessary suffering in the world, as the prophets were. But hope – the vision of the marvellous things that are possible –

is usually a more effective agent of change than criticism, satire or solemn denunciation. Dr Martin Luther King had much to say about the injustices suffered by black people, but he is remembered chiefly for his dream of sons of former slaves and sons of former slave owners in Georgia sitting down together at the table of brotherhood, of the state of Mississippi transformed into an oasis of freedom and justice, and little black children and little white children in Alabama joining hands as brothers and sisters. Human beings need to dream, to celebrate and to sing.

The best known biblical vision of world peace is found in two places, in Isaiah and in Micah (Isa 2:2-4; Mic 4:1-4), with almost identical wording. These two prophets were close contemporaries. Either could have copied from the other, or perhaps both were quoting a popular hymn of the time. It is a dream of the temple mount, "the mountain of the LORD's house" exalted so that it becomes the highest, that is the focal point for the whole world. All the nations will stream to it, acknowledging the God of Israel and ready to learn his ways. In this way God will become the judge and arbiter among the nations and there will be universal peace. Micah makes a beautiful addition to the picture:

"but they shall all sit under their own vines and under their own fig trees,

and no one shall make them afraid." (NRSV)

This is capped only by Zechariah who, imagining Judah under the stable rule of a just king, and perhaps deliberately rephrasing Micah, says (Zech 3:10, NRSV):

"On that day...you shall invite each other to come under your vine and fig tree."

This vision of one God enlightening the whole world and teaching it to live according to his laws must have seemed a wild dream in the time of Isaiah and Micah, but in the course of centuries it has revealed itself as a real possibility. Those principles that were taught in the temple in Jerusalem are now known throughout the world and have made, in spite of many setbacks, some contribution to world peace. Already in the time of Christ, Judaism was a growing faith with wide influence throughout the Roman Empire and beyond. Many people were drawn by its simplicity and moral integrity. Soon it was overtaken by its daughter faith Christianity, which eventually became the religion of the whole empire and spread beyond the borders of that empire to the east and the west. Then came Islam, another offshoot of the religion of Israel that displaced Christianity in North Africa and the Middle East and brought a unified and advanced civilisation not only to that area but further East to the Indian subcontinent and beyond.

The situation was transformed again in the late Middle Ages by the discovery of America, and the opening up of new trade routes. The balance of power shifted in favour of the Christian nations, and Christianity went on to become a worldwide faith protected by the European empires. The churches especially of the nineteenth and early twentieth centuries enthusiastically embraced the challenge of worldwide mission. In doing so they exported not only the Christian faith but also a whole European way of life. They saw themselves as educating, civilizing and pacifying the rest of the world.

Perhaps the high point of this movement was the great International Missionary Conference in Edinburgh in 1910. As with many human enterprises, its chief effect was different from its original aim. In one sense it was a new beginning: it was the main impetus, for Protestants at least, of the ecumenical movement that has so changed the face of the Christian churches. But as far as the Christianizing of the whole world is concerned, 1910 now looks more like the beginning of the end. The slogan that rallied all the missionary societies and inspired them to work together was "the evangelization of the world in this generation". Today the world has certainly been evangelized in the sense that there are now Christian churches in every country, but it has not been evangelized *successfully* in the way that the leaders in 1910 probably envisaged.

Only four years after this conference Europe, the continent from which Christian culture had been exported to the rest of the world, was engulfed in a disastrous war. It left many people disillusioned with traditional beliefs and values and paved the way for a much more questioning, sceptical and secular society. That war also brought the Russian revolution that introduced militant atheistic Communism over a wide area of Europe and Asia. The Communist ideology spread into many countries, eventually leading to the complete closure to Christian missionaries of China, the most populous nation in the world.

Later in the twentieth century came the breaking up of the European empires. Countries to which missionaries had enjoyed free access became independent and able to restrict or refuse entry to them. Many of these former colonies reasserted their own cultural and religious heritage. Islam, Buddhism and Hinduism, as well as the traditions of China and Japan, are now forces to be reckoned with in the global political and religious scene.

At the same time, economic developments led to massive immigration into Western European countries, so that today Western Christians have to think of people of other faiths no longer as faraway "heathen" to whom they send missionaries but as neighbours on the same street and colleagues in the same workplace. Even many of those whose cultural heritage is Christian now hold to an eclectic spirituality that mixes Christianity with elements of Buddhism and Hinduism. We live in a market-place of faiths and world views in which "winning the world for Christ" seems to many people not only unrealistic but arrogant. We increasingly recognise that the other great faith traditions contribute as much to peace as Christianity. We recognise the other side of the coin too, that some elements in Christianity can contribute to division and war.

Probably the nearest we have today to the ideal of the whole world uniting around one "teaching" is the philosophy expressed in such things as the United Nations' Universal Declaration of Human Rights, the Geneva Convention, and the International Criminal Court. There is a feeling that, whatever people's creed or culture, there are certain basic humanitarian principles on which everyone agrees, and that on the basis of these principles there can be a peaceful world. But today even this consensus is being questioned. It is argued that the ideology behind "human rights" is a Western liberal perception of human life and society, a kind of secularised Christianity owing much to the American Declaration of Independence and not necessarily appropriate to other cultures. With the resurgence of religion as a strong and often divisive force, even this foundation is beginning to look rather shaky.

It seems that the path to world peace today is a much more difficult and complex one. People of different faiths and cultures have to strive for justice in their own terms and at the same time learn to understand, respect and compromise with each other. Yet with all the differences there is an underlying convergence of the major religious traditions, together with modern secular liberalism, towards the recognition that there is something about the vision of Isaiah and Micah that is fundamentally right: that peace is both an ideal and a possibility.

Another vision in the Book of Isaiah that has been a great inspiration is that of the righteous king (Isa 11:1-9):

"A shoot shall come out from the stock of Jesse, and a branch shall grow out of his roots.

The spirit of the LORD shall rest on him

The spirit of wisdom and understanding,

the spirit of counsel and might,

the spirit of knowledge and the fear of the LORD..." (NRSV)

Jesse features in the story about Samuel going to his house in Bethlehem to find the future king (1 Sam 16). That king was David, the founder of a dynasty that ruled in Jerusalem for centuries and was believed to be ordained by God as an eternal kingdom. This passage in Isaiah may be a later addition from a time after that kingdom had been destroyed. On the other hand, it could be expressing the prophet's disillusionment with David's successors and possibly his conviction, in the shadow of the Assyrian threat, that the kingdom was about to be destroyed. It is a vision of God going back to the very beginning, not even to David but to where David came from, like a re-play of Samuel's journey to the house of Jesse to begin all over again and find a worthy king.

Although the connection with the birth of Jesus in Bethlehem is unavoidable for Christians, we have to imagine what it must have meant to the prophet and his first hearers. It is not so much a prediction as an aspiration: the dream of a better king, a king under whose rule there would be real justice, a realm where bribery, corruption and favouritism would be no more.

A reign like this would create harmony, and here the prophet begins to wax lyrical. He sees the wolf lying down with the lamb: perhaps a figure of speech for harmony between the strong and the weak in society. He sees a child playing by the snake's nest. Perhaps that too is figurative: the "snakes" in society who threaten the safety of the vulnerable and innocent will lose their power to do harm. Or it could be that in his imagination he sees harmony in human society spreading out to the whole of nature. We are reminded of the close connection, of which we are more than ever aware today, between the behaviour of human beings and the fate of the natural world. In this vision the whole world will be filled with the knowledge of God and become as sacred as the temple mount in Jerusalem.

This belief that peace and justice will be established when the right person is in charge has been a theme of human hopes in many of the world's cultures. At the time of the birth of Jesus people in the Roman Empire were hailing Augustus Caesar as the bringer of a new era of peace for the whole world. The titles given to Jesus by the early Christians – the Lord, Son of God, King of Kings, Prince of Peace and so on – were the same titles that were given to the Emperor. On the lips of the followers of Jesus, they were an assertion that his way, and not the way of Empire, was the way that true peace would come.

The history of the twentieth century, perhaps more than any other, is littered with leaders who were seen as saviours, almost all of whom turned out to be disappointing and often disastrous: Stalin, Hitler, Mussolini, Mao Tse Tung, Pol Pot and the leaders of numerous Communist countries and newly independent African nations. Some of these are still with us today. We have to ask whether the whole idea of peace, justice and prosperity coming through one person is an illusion. For Christians, the view of Jesus Christ as Saviour of the world is tempered by the insight that it is through his genuine believers and followers, the "salt of the earth" and the "leaven in the lump" that the world is being redeemed. Salvation does not come through having the right leader: the people as a whole needs to be transformed.

There is yet another vision of hope in the Book of Isaiah, this time in the latest part of the book (Isa 65:17-25), which comes from a time when Jerusalem had been destroyed and restored and was once again struggling with its problems. This vision is perhaps the most inspiring of all. It starts with what looks like a cosmic statement:

"I am making a new earth and new heavens... Be glad and rejoice for ever in what I create. The new Jerusalem I make will be full of joy, and her people will be happy."

This is the origin of the phrase "the New Jerusalem" that is taken up in the New Testament Book of Revelation (Rev 21) and has become a stock expression of utopian aspirations in modern times. But while the vision in the Book of Revelation is of a re-creating of the whole world, in this passage in Isaiah the cosmic vision at the beginning soon becomes "earthed" in the actual city of Jerusalem. Unlike the New Jerusalem of Revelation where "death will be no more", this one will be an earthly city subject to the natural conditions of earthly life, but better:

"Babies will no longer die in infancy, and all people will live out their lifespan. Those who live to be a hundred will be considered young. To die before that would be a sign that I had punished them. People will build houses and live in them themselves – they will not be used by someone else. They will plant vineyards and enjoy the wine – it will not be drunk by others."

Here the prophet surely strikes a chord with the hopes and dreams of today, portraying the kind of world for which we still strive and hope.

After this description he again waxes lyrical, echoing the language of that earlier passage about the wolf and the lamb feeding together and the holy mountain where there will be no hurting or destroying.

In this vision of the city there is no mention of a king: by the time it was written the hope of restoring the monarchy in the line of David had probably been given up. More strangely, apart from the reference to "my holy mountain" there is no mention of a temple either. Just a little further on, in the final chapter of the book, we find the whole idea of a temple being questioned:

"The LORD says, 'Heaven is my throne and the earth is my footstool. What kind of house, then, could you build for me, what kind of place for me to live in? I myself created the whole universe!'" (Isa 66:1-2)

Perhaps here we are hearing the voice of a radical prophet soon after the return from the exile in Babylon and the re-constituting of the Jewish community. The community leaders and other prophets – people like Ezra, Nehemiah, Haggai and Zechariah – were worrying about rebuilding the temple, but this prophet was questioning the need for it altogether. The glory and the holiness here are expressed not in the king or the temple but in the whole people in its life with God.

In the picture of the New Jerusalem in the Book of Revelation there is no temple, "because its temple is the Lord God Almighty and the Lamb" (Rev 21:22). When God truly makes his dwelling-place with humanity there will be no need for temples. Religions erect temples and churches with walls to mark them off from the ordinary world outside so that they can be "the house of God". But in reality God is present everywhere, all ground is holy, and God is present in the whole human race, not just in kings and priests. So perhaps here in the Book of Isaiah, and even more in Revelation, we have the beginnings of a kind of secularism: not the secularism that excludes God, but the kind that breaks down the distinction between the religious and the secular because it sees this world in its plain physicality infused everywhere with the divine presence.

Once again the New Testament vision of the New Jerusalem is foreshadowed:

"No longer will the sun be your light by day,
or the moon be your light by night;
I, the LORD, will be your eternal light;
the light of my glory will shine on you." (Isa 60:19)

So in the Hebrew prophets there is this constant theme of facing failure and disaster and believing in a new beginning, the theme expressed in the New Testament as death and resurrection. The Israelites generally during the period in which their Scriptures were written, had no concept of a glorified life beyond death. However, here and there we do find a hint of the resurrection of the dead and a world in which death will be no more. The strongest of these hints is perhaps in the Book of Isaiah:

"Here on Mount Zion the LORD Almighty will prepare a banquet for all the nations of the world – a banquet of the richest food and the finest wine. Here he will suddenly remove the cloud of sorrow that has been hanging over all the nations. The Sovereign LORD will destroy death for ever! He will wipe away the tears from everyone's eyes..." (Isa 25:6-8)

In such a passage as this we begin to wonder whether all the prophets were *just* concerned about change in this present world. As in Isaiah's vision of the wolf lying down with the lamb, we seem to be on the cusp of a breakthrough from metaphor into something more literal, the belief in a transformation of creation itself. This breakthrough comes in the type of literature known as "apocalyptic", exemplified chiefly by the books of Daniel in the Jewish Scriptures and Revelation in the New Testament.

The second part of the Book of Daniel is a series of dreams predicting the rise and fall of empires and the final establishment of the kingdom of God. The visions are highly symbolic and at the same time topical in a way that is now hard for us to follow. "Apocalyptic" writings are rather different from prophecy, though a development of it. They are written to comfort and reassure people suffering extreme oppression, and they are in a kind of code that would be understood by their readers while hiding their real meaning from the authorities. The Book of Daniel seems to refer to the crisis of 168 BC, when a Syrian king defiled the temple and tried to abolish the Jewish religion: events which brought about the rebellion led by Judas Maccabeus and the short period of Jewish independence before the Romans took over.

In the seventh chapter Daniel dreams of four fierce beasts appearing one after the other, and then of a cosmic court of judgment in which God gives power and authority to a human figure, "one like a son of man". The four beasts are interpreted as four great empires – probably Assyria, Babylon, Persia and Greece – and the human figure represents "the people of the Supreme God" (presumably the devout Jewish believers) whose rule will last forever.

Apocalyptic literature represents the aspirations of people facing such a desperate situation that it seems that only a spectacular divine intervention on a cosmic scale can save them. Tired of dashed hopes and disappointed aspirations, some people began to talk about an ideal world that would only come after the cataclysmic destruction of this world. The hope of change was transferred from this world to an eternal world beyond history. A belief like this has boosted people's courage and hopes in times of severe oppression, but in established Christian societies it has often become an incentive to opt out of concern for this world and transpose all idealistic hopes to heaven. In modern times it has also provided a happy hunting ground for those who are constantly looking out for signs of the "second coming" in contemporary events, mostly in the "Holy Land", while ignoring the major world-wide issues of poverty, injustice and war. At the same time we must remember that this apocalyptic writing was originally a response to a sense of extreme injustice countered by a hope of justice beyond this world.

11

The Call and the Cost

The story of Isaiah's vision in the Temple (Isa 6) has entered deeply into the language and imagination of Christians. It was a mystical experience: Isaiah saw the LORD sitting on his throne attended by seraphim – winged serpent-like figures – who were calling out to each other, "Holy, holy, holy is the LORD of hosts; the whole earth is full of his glory" (NRSV) – words that are familiar to Christians through liturgy and hymns. This was perhaps a hymn being sung by the temple singers at the time. The sanctuary would be filled with smoke both from the incense and from the animal sacrifices burning on the altar. But to Isaiah in his state of exaltation it was all one, and the whole temple seemed to shake. The overwhelming sense of a holy presence made him aware of his un-holiness. He was fearful, because he had seen the LORD, something that no mortal was meant to survive.

We assume that this passage is the kind of "call story" that other prophets had, but it is unusual in that it does not come at the beginning of the book. It could be that Isaiah had already begun to preach, but that this vision struck him with the reali-sation of how unfit he was, as a mortal, to speak for the holy God whose glory fills the whole earth. Perhaps that is why he said:

"There is no hope for me! I am doomed because every word that passes my lips is sinful, and I live among a people whose every word is sinful."

It is a huge responsibility to speak to the public on serious issues, and we all know the harm that can be done (not to mention the tedium that can be generated!) by someone whose motivation is just that they like the sound of their own voice and the opportunity of a platform or a pulpit from which to expound their opinions.

Once Isaiah realised the unfitness of his lips to speak for God, his only hope was to be convinced of a drastic cleansing, and this was achieved by his lips being burnt with a coal from the altar. He now had confidence that by God's grace he could speak. And so when he heard God saying to the heavenly council, "Whom shall I send? Who will be our messenger?" he knew that this was meant for him, and responded, "I will go! Send me!"

This story has often been used by preachers as a classic account of a call to ministry or missionary service. The preacher presents the people with the challenge of work needing to be done in some distant place, and invites them to say (in the traditional words) "Here am I, send me!" What is often overlooked is that for Isaiah it was not so much a call as a warning. God's response to his offer was to say:

"Make the minds of these people dull, their ears deaf, and their eyes blind, so that they cannot see or hear or understand. If they did, they might turn to me and be healed."

It is as if God is saying, "Go and preach if you like, but they won't listen to you!" God tells him that his preaching will be positively counter-productive: every word he says will harden their hearts further.

This realistic, rather cynical view of the role of a prophet is comparatively rare in the Hebrew Scriptures. There is something of it in the Book of Ezekiel, where the prophet hears God saying to him:

"To them you are nothing more than an entertainer singing love songs or playing a harp. They listen to all your words and don't obey a single one of them." (Ezek 33:32)

Many a preacher down through the ages has felt the truth of those words after preaching his heart out, saying something he felt was really important to say, and then being told "That was nice!", or "You have a lovely voice"! It can be even worse for women preachers, who are more likely to be complimented on their dress or their hair style! There is a story of a preacher whose deacons approached him to complain that he was preaching the same sermon about "love your neighbour" every week. A good theme, they said, but did he not have any other sermons? His response was, "But you haven't started doing *that* yet!" The same kind of thing happens in the world of popular music: how many people who listen to protest songs take notice of their message rather than just enjoying the tune?

Isaiah's words re-emerge in the New Testament. There is a story in Matthew's Gospel about the disciples asking Jesus why he spoke in parables (Matt 13:10-15). His response is that the parables are also in a sense riddles: they hide the truth from those who are too dull to see it. Jesus picks up the words of Isaiah and tells his disciples that the majority of the people listen without understanding and look without perceiving. They have closed their eyes and their ears so that they cannot turn to the truth and be healed. Here, as in Isaiah, Jesus seems to be implying that this effect is deliberate on his part: probably a striking figure of speech to convey how inevitable it is.

However passionately we may feel about something, we always have to face the reality that most human beings for most of the time are depressingly insensitive. I remember the experience I sometimes had as a young man of being deeply moved by a film, and when it ended and the lights came up I was amazed at how the ushers could go around tidying and cleaning with a look of utter boredom on their faces! To me, the evening had been a heart-moving, challenging and possibly life-changing experience, but to them it was just another shift. I used to think, "Even if they have already seen the film several times this week, how can they not be moved by it?" As I look back now on my idealistic youth, I have to be more honest. Books and films have moved me and inspired me many times over the years, but how much difference have they actually made? Being emotionally affected is easy, but making a real practical change in one's life is a different thing, and it happens very rarely.

This insensitivity is encountered by anyone with something urgent to say. An unwelcome message, no matter how logical, urgent or apparently irrefutable, can create its own resistance. If people do not want to accept the implications of what they hear, there is no limit to the arguments they will use to dismiss the message or to discredit the messenger. This is apparent today in the "debate" about whether human activity is causing serious climate change. In the face of the almost a hundred percent of leading scientists who believe the evidence is overwhelming, the strength of some people's resistance is astounding. It is understandable that some people express doubts about some of the evidence: this is natural, and it makes for a reasonable debate. But a surprising number of people close their minds to the whole idea, label and ridicule those who talk about it as "green freaks" or "panic merchants", or declare that the whole thing is a hoax.

Isaiah's question and the answer he received are very relevant to our situation today. When he asked how long this must go on, the answer was:

"Until the cities are ruined and empty – until the houses are uninhabited – until the land itself is a desolate waste."

If this is the case, and there is no hope at all, we may well ask what is the point of all our preaching and campaigning. Humanity is doomed anyway, so why waste our efforts? And yet it has often been found in human life that people wake up when it is almost, but not quite, too late. There comes a time when the most closed minds can no longer ignore the unwelcome truth, and something is done to salvage the situation at the last moment. The biblical threats of judgment are never irreversible predictions: they are wake-up calls, urging the people to change their ways.

The account of the vision ends on a note that is at least slightly optimistic. In fact, some commentators think it is incongruous, and suggest it was added later by another writer. After likening the destruction to a tree being felled and even its stump being burned, it is implied that the stump will survive, and the chapter ends with a little note (in NRSV): "The holy seed is its stump". This is not necessarily a contradiction: it chimes in with statements later in the book about the faithful few who will remain and become the seed of new hope (Isa 10:21-22; 11:11). The Good News Bible interprets it with a bracketed note: "The stump represents a new beginning for God's people".

At one point it seems that Isaiah decided to remain silent for a while and simply wait for God to prove the truth of what he had been preaching:

"You, my disciples, are to guard and preserve the messages that God has given me. The LORD has hidden himself from his people, but I trust him and place my hope in him." (Isa 8:16-17)

Here we may well have a hint of how the words of the prophets came to be written down and eventually to become Scripture.

The second Isaiah took up this theme of the blindness and deafness of the people in a very different situation. In the original Isaiah's time people seemed incapable of hearing the warning of judgment to come: in this new situation it was the *good* news they were unable to hear. The prophet says:

"Is anyone more blind than my servant,
more deaf than the messenger I send?
Israel, you have seen so much,
but what has it meant to you?
You have ears to hear with,
but what have you really heard?" (Isa 42:18-20)

They were unable to see that it was God who gave them into the hands of their enemies as a judgment, and now they are unable to see that God is restoring them. The prophet urges them to see and understand their special place in history, to be witnesses to the God who is Lord of the whole world (Isa 43:8-10):

"People of Israel, you are my witnesses;

I chose you to be my servant, so that you would know me and believe in me and understand that I am the only God."

This is said in the context of a kind of cosmic law court in which God is presenting his case to the nations. The call is to "bring forth" the witnesses and assemble all the nations. We can almost hear the usher's voice echoing through the corridors:

"Summon my people to court.

They have eyes, but they are blind;

they have ears, but they are deaf!"

The people do not understand what the whole thing is about. Their very history proclaims God, but in their state of ignorance they are in a sense only *exhibits* in this trial. If they are to be real *witnesses* they must understand and believe. Perhaps there is a suggestion here of the paradoxical place of religious communities in the world. Their very existence, and the way in which they emerged and have survived, is a kind of witness to the divine presence in history, but this often happens not because of their virtues but in spite of their failings. The effectiveness of the witness is not entirely dependent on how good the witnesses are, or how efficient they are in spreading their message, or even how well they themselves understand it.

In Western culture today the knowledge of Jesus and his ways is not confined to Christians. Whatever people think of organised religion or of the churches, there is a widespread perception of what Christianity is supposed to be about, and sometimes people who make no claim to practise Christianity have a clearer idea of what it means than those who do. The challenge to those who belong to the community of faith is to see, understand and actually believe what they profess to believe. This is tellingly illustrated in the irony of the New Testament story of the Magi coming from a far country to look for the new-born King of the Jews (Matt 2:1-11). The scholars can consult their Scriptures and guide the visitors to the right place, but it is the strangers from a far country who actually *go* there! So today faith communities are often the custodians of a radical message that inspires other people while they themselves are failing to perceive it.

For some of the prophets, the message they had to proclaim was costly to themselves. Hosea's call story begins with God saying to him:

"Go and get married; your wife will be unfaithful, and your children will be just like her. In the same way, my people have left me and become unfaithful." (Hos 1:2)

This could be interpreted in different ways. It could be an example of the symbolic actions that prophets sometimes used to reinforce their message: perhaps Hosea went through a form of marriage with a cultic prostitute in order to symbolise Israel's unfaithfulness to her God. But the intensity of the emotion in some parts of the book suggests that it could be retrospective reflection on real life. Hosea looks back over his turbulent domestic life and interprets Israel's relationship with the LORD in the light of his own experience and emotions.

Jeremiah, more than most prophets, suffered persecution and inner anguish. There are passages in his book sometimes known as the "confessions of Jeremiah", where the prophet expresses the depth of his own feeling:

"I wish my head were a well of water,

and my eyes a fountain of tears,

so that I could cry day and night

for my people who have been killed."

He longs for an escape:

"I wish I had a place to stay in the desert

where I could get away from my people." (Jer 9:1-2)

He seems at several times to have been the victim of plots and death threats, and often calls upon God in anger:

"Remember how I came to you and spoke on their behalf, so that you would not deal with them in anger. But now, LORD, let their children starve to death; let them be killed in war ... Do not forgive their evil or pardon their sin." (Jer 18:20-23)

Far from delighting in his role as "a Jeremiah", he complains of it:

"Why did my mother bring me into the world? I have to quarrel and argue with everyone in the land. I have not lent any money or borrowed any; yet everyone curses me." (Jer 15:10)

He complains that God has let him down:

"You spoke to me, and I listened to every word. I belong to you, LORD God Almighty, and so your words filled my heart with joy and happiness... Do you intend to disappoint me like a stream that goes dry in the summer?" (Jer 15:16-18)

Yet through it all he cannot escape the compulsion to speak out his message:

"But when I say, 'I will forget the LORD
and no longer speak in his name',
then your message is like a fire
burning deep within me.
I try my best to hold it in,
but can no longer keep it back." (Jer 20:9)

His despair is sometimes suicidal:

"Why was I born?
Was it only to have trouble and sorrow,
to end my life in disgrace?" (Jer 20:18)

In the second part of Isaiah there is a series of passages that make particular reference to the LORD's "servant", a character who, like many features of poetry, is difficult to pin down. Sometimes it seems to represent the whole people in its mission to the world. At other times the speech is in the first person, seeming to imply that it may be the prophet himself. At other times it seems to be the people speaking about someone else. Because of their similarity to each other these passages are often referred to as the "Servant Songs".

The first (Isa 42:1-7) begins:

"The LORD says,
Here is my servant, whom I strengthen –

the one I have chosen, with whom I am pleased."

The mission of this servant is to "bring justice to every nation": a magnificent vision of God's justice as being for the whole world. The servant will achieve this not by force and aggression, but quietly – "he will not shout or raise his voice, or make loud speeches in the streets" – and persistently – "he will not lose hope or courage". God addresses the servant:

"I, the LORD, have called you and given you power
to see that justice is done on earth.
Through you I will make a covenant with all peoples,
through you I will bring light to the nations."

The "covenant" was the LORD's special relationship with Israel as his holy people: here we are presented with the vision of this relationship, this holiness, being extended to all peoples.

In the second song (Isa 49:1-7) it is the Servant himself who speaks initially:

"Before I was born, the LORD chose me
and appointed me to be his servant...
He said to me, 'Israel, you are my servant,
because of you, people will praise me.'"

Here the servant is evidently the whole nation of Israel, and yet a little further on he seems to be an individual with a special mission to Israel and the world:

"The LORD said to me,
'I have a greater task for you, my servant.
Not only will you restore to greatness
the people of Israel who have survived,
but I will also make you a light to the nations –
so that all the world may be saved."

These words are addressed to:

"the one who is deeply despised,
who is hated by the nations
and is the servant of rulers."

The next one (Isa 50:4-9) sounds very much like the self-reflections of a prophet, reminiscent of the "confessions" of Jeremiah. The speaker talks of having been given "the tongue of a teacher" (NRSV) and having his ears awakened to hear the message from God. He faces opposition and persecution, but says:

"I bared my back to those who beat me.

I did not stop them when they insulted me,

when they pulled out the hairs of my beard

and spat in my face."

Yet after this suffering he is not disgraced but vindicated. Here we have a foretaste of the last, longest and best known of the "servant songs". Familiar to most Christians as "Isaiah 53", it actually begins towards the end of chapter 52:

"The LORD says,

'My servant will succeed in his task,

he will be highly honoured ...'"

But this prospering and exalted servant faces extreme suffering:

"Many people were shocked when they saw him,

he was so disfigured that he hardly looked human."

The rulers of nations will see this servant and be astonished by something never seen before. In spite of having "no dignity or beauty to make us take notice of him" and being "despised" and "rejected", he will be given "a place among the great and powerful".

In a sense this is the culmination of the theme of failure that was first raised in the first Isaiah's vision in the temple. The messenger now is not only ignored but condemned and persecuted, and yet it is somehow through that very thing that his mission is accomplished:

"But because of our sins he was wounded,

beaten because of the evil we did.

We are healed by the punishment he suffered,

made whole by the blows he received."

Much is left unsaid in this poem. It raises the same questions we have already seen in the others, as to whether the servant is the nation or an individual, and if an individual, who? The statement that the servant was unprepossessing and despised is reminiscent of the "shoot out of the stock of Jesse" that appears after the mighty trees have been cut down (Isa 10:33 – 11:1). It suggests that the person referred to may be a king. Perhaps he is the king of Israel, deposed and humiliated by the Babylonians. Or perhaps he is the prophet despised by his own people. As with all great poetry, its very ambiguity opens it up to multiple interpretations and speaks to the heart more than to the head.

It is hard for many Christians to read this passage without seeing in it the doctrine of substitutionary atonement which is the standard interpretation of the death of Jesus preached by a certain kind of Protestant evangelicalism. This states that because God could not violate his own justice human sin could not be forgiven unless someone was punished. Therefore God sent his own Son Jesus to take the punishment in our place: our guilt was transferred to him and his righteousness is transferred to us if we believe in him. But the New Testament offers a number of different ways of thinking of the meaning of the death of Jesus, and in reading this passage in Isaiah we have to be very careful, as often in the Bible, to notice what it says and what it does not say.

What is being described in this passage is a dramatic example of the common human experience that it is often the most innocent people who suffer because of what is wrong in society. This is seen everywhere in the world today. We can look at the assassinations of brave, good people who have stood up for justice, or at the horrific wounds suffered by ordinary people through terrorist attacks, or the young lives that are cut off in war, or the swollen bellies and emaciated limbs of starving children, and we have to acknowledge that these things happen because of the kind of world we have created by our greed, prejudice and false values: they reflect the worst side of ourselves back to us. Of these people we can truly say that "because of our sins" they are wounded, and "beaten because of the evil we did". And there is also a sense in which this suffering can produce healing. A tragedy or an atrocity can sometimes be the catalyst for a change. The unjust killing of a highly respected person, or the death of young men and women in war, can shock the world into a resolve that this must not happen again. Though it seems to take an enormous amount of suffering to achieve a small improvement in the world, there is a glimmer of hope that people do not suffer and die in vain.

The connection with substitutionary atonement seems to be reinforced by the statements that:

"the LORD made the punishment fall on him,

the punishment all of us deserved"

and:

"The LORD says,

'It was my will that he should suffer;

his death was a sacrifice to bring forgiveness.'"

But in reading these we have to remember that in ancient Jewish thinking the almighty God was thought to be responsible for everything that happened, good or bad. We could also interpret these statements as showing that if, as the previous Servant Songs have implied, justice is to be established in the world not through force but through gentleness, then the LORD does approve of the Servant's willingness to suffer, because it is the only way.

We must beware of drawing the wrong conclusions from this passage in Isaiah by reading traditional Christian doctrine into it or simply seeing it as a prediction of the suffering and death of Jesus. We do not know the person or the events the prophet was referring to, but we can be sure that the words had their own meaning in their own time. Having said that, this poem has acquired a far deeper and richer meaning in the course of history. Jews have seen in it a picture of themselves as a people somehow chosen to suffer as God's witnesses to the world. Christians have seen it as a portrait of Jesus dying for the world's salvation.

Like many of the prophets, Jesus encountered opposition and eventually death for his preaching. He anticipated this: as he began his journey towards Jerusalem, he said with a note of resignation, "it is not right for a prophet to be killed anywhere except in Jerusalem" (Luke 13:33). And just as some of the earlier prophets, like Hosea and Jeremiah, had expressed their message with their lives, so Jesus expressed his message in his death. This insight is expressed in the way Paul and other early Christian preachers said little about his teachings or the details of his life, but concentrated on presenting his death and resurrection as God's ultimate message to the world. As John's Gospel puts it, Jesus does not just preach the word of God: he *is* the Word (John 1:14).

12

Prophecy for Today

There is something deeply moving, hopeful and at the same time depressing about Edmund Sears' well-known Christmas hymn "It came upon the midnight clear", with its plea to the world's warring peoples to "hush the noise" and "hear the angels sing", and its declaration that the day will come:

"when peace will over all the earth
its ancient splendours fling,
and the whole world send back the song
which now the angels sing."

The depressing thing about it is that we have been singing these words since 1849. In the meantime we have seen two world wars and all the other horrors of the twentieth century. The twenty-first century began with the usual resolutions and even a mood of euphoria in some quarters, but is has shown no sign as yet of being any better for humanity as a whole. The "9/11" attack on America in 2001 had a huge impact not only on the United States but on the world wide political picture. With the pursuit of terrorists in Afghanistan, Pakistan and other countries, the war in Iraq, unrest in the Arab world, the tragic ongoing civil war in Syria and the cooling of relations between Russia and the West, peace seems to be as far off as ever. Not only in unstable and conflict-ridden societies, but in the comparative safety of North America and Western Europe, we live in the constant awareness of terrorism.

In addition, the past few years have seen an increasing concern about immigration, often showing itself in open xenophobia, prejudice and hate crimes. Anxiety about the influx of Eastern Europeans was a contributory factor to the referendum in which Britain decided to leave the European Union. It has now been overtaken by the vast flow of refugees from the civil war in Syria and the buck-passing arguments about where they will be allowed to settle. Poverty and insecurity are driving many people from other countries too into desperate attempts to enter Europe, and at the same time lining the pockets of unscrupulous people-traffickers. In America, a similar anxiety about Mexican immigrants from one direction and fear of Islamic terrorism from another is fuelling the rise of xenophobic and racist elements.

Immigration, whether by "economic migrants" or refugees, is an issue that will not go away. In fact, with continuing unrest in many countries, extreme inequality, and the threat of climate change, we can expect it to increase. Unless some long term approach is found, it will lead to more and more tragic suffering and death. We seem to be heading for a world in which the struggle for survival will override all the peaceable and neighbourly values of civilisation. Communities and individuals will build up defences, close their borders and care less and less for the welfare of others.

The Victorian era that gave birth to that hymn was one of optimism. The advance of science and technology was improving the conditions of life for many. Europeans were confident in their Christian civilisation and busy exporting it to the rest of the world. There was a feeling that humanity was becoming more enlightened year by year and the kingdom of God was being built on earth.

People often say that the First World War delivered the death blow to this optimism, but it has emerged from time to time in other ways. Those of us who were growing up in Britain in the years following the Second World War had a sense of progress. Poverty was being eliminated by economic recovery and the cushion of the Welfare State. Health care was available free to all. Young people from poor homes had educational opportunities and career prospects their parents never knew. Full employment had returned and the hardship of the 1920s and 1930s seemed like the memory of a bad dream. Miners and factory workers were acquiring smart modern houses and cars, and having holidays abroad. There was a feeling that the younger generation would have a better life than their parents and that their children's lives would be better still.

The mood has changed in the past few decades. Many young people now feel they have only unemployment or low paid menial jobs to look forward to. More people than ever are going to university, but a degree is no longer an open door to a professional career or even to a job at all. The Health Service is plagued with problems, benefits are being reduced, and the security of pensions and care for elderly people is under threat. There is a general feeling that the best days are over. There are places in the world where hope is still alive – relatively poor communities that are taking their situation in hand and aiming to build something better, countries that are beginning to emerge from endemic poverty and see a better future ahead – but in the West the talk is all about austerity and continuing economic and social problems.

As a result of this many people are becoming alienated from society and denying any responsibility for it because it seems to have nothing to offer them. They are not bothering to vote because they cannot see what difference it makes. Others are embracing a kind of spirituality that detaches itself from the concerns of society and seeks personal salvation. This may take the form of the kind of evangelical Christianity that ensures believers of their place in heaven and has little interest in what is going on in the world. It may be expressed in Islamic extremism that turns its back on Western culture and hopes to find salvation in being part of a great holy war. Others may turn to other-worldly Eastern mysticism, or to the more secular programmes geared more to individual development and success than to community. Those who have something of the spirit of the biblical prophets today and talk of real change in this world as a possibility are likely to be dismissed as unrealistic idealists, out of touch with reality and politically irrelevant.

At the same time we have to recognise that most of us in the West still have a comfortable life with luxuries beyond anything enjoyed by earlier generations. By world standards we are the rich. This faces us with the uncomfortable thought that the parts of the prophets' preaching that most apply to us may not be the bright images of a better life but the warnings of judgment. If we are to be part of the prophetic dreams of a better world, we must at least recognise that there is a cost.

There is some recognition of this in the way many young people today are offering time and energy to the service of people in greater need than themselves. Some older people too are "down-sizing" to a simpler lifestyle that makes fewer demands on the environment and reduces the exploitation of their fellow human beings. People of all ages are turning to the kind of politics that aims for real change in the balance of rich and poor. But these are a minority, because to most people it seems unrealistic, and politicians who espouse it are labelled as "unelectable".

This is why we need the perspective of the biblical prophets. Most of us in the Western world need to be challenged about inequality because we benefit from it, and when it is built on unethical foundations it must eventually lead to disaster. At the same time, we need the prophets' hopeful visions that were not of *another* world but of *this* world being better – the vision of a society built on foundations of justice, compassion and right values.

Europe and North America share a culture that has been shaped by the Christian faith, and the preaching of the Hebrew prophets behind it. However, in many ways Christianity has become part of the problem. "Faith" has become a set of beliefs to which people are expected to subscribe so as to be regarded as "orthodox". Having the "orthodox" beliefs may have very little to do with real life. In one's political views or business activities, the norms that prevail are shaped by factors other than faith. The "realities" of the market make the rules in business, and putting the interests of one's own country or class before those of others is what makes the rules in politics. This is very different from the way things were for the early Christians and for the prophets before them. When the first Christians said, "Jesus is Lord", they were not expressing some theological doctrine about the status of Jesus in the spiritual realm. They were saying of Jesus what subjects of the Roman Empire were expected to say of Caesar. The Book of Revelation paints a portrait of the kind of totalitarian regime that the Roman Empire had it in itself to be: a world in which everyone had to bear the "mark of the beast" before they could buy or sell (Rev 13:16-17). For the early Christians the statement "Jesus is Lord" was a costly one to make: many paid with their lives for refusing to call the Emperor a god.

Some writers compare the power of the United States, or of global capitalism generally, with this totalitarian regime. There is, however, one difference. Most of the leading nations involved in the global market are democracies. Government is not imposed by powerful individuals or hereditary establishments, but elected by the people. The people, of course, are deeply influenced and often misinformed by the media, which are controlled by large companies and wealthy individuals. However, this does not alter the fact that ordinary people are free to express opinions, and these opinions are often narrow, selfish and xenophobic. The struggle for justice is not just a struggle against powerful individuals and institutions: it faces the challenge of the dark side of human nature as a whole. The increase in prejudice and violence against immigrants and other minorities in Europe, the xenophobic attitudes in Britain that in some quarters seem to have been given licence by the decision to leave the European Union, the rise of Islamic extremism and the exaggerated Islamophobic reaction to it, and the surge of extremist views in a large proportion of the population of the United States, have created a situation in which many despair of seeing any progress towards a more just and peaceful world. In such a situation it is tempting to retreat into either pietism or apocalyptic. The pietistic answer is that this world is bad and always will be, and that the hope religion offers is of heaven after we die. The apocalyptic answer, in Christian terms, is that the world is destined to get progressively worse until Christ returns on the clouds of heaven and the whole world as we know it comes to an end. It takes courage and faith to hold on to the hope of the prophets that repentance, i.e. a radical change of attitude leading to renewal, is possible *within this world*.

To be true to this faith and the spirit of early Christianity, Christians today need to say: we obey Jesus, not the market; our first allegiance is to the kingdom of God, not to our country. This of course is costly. Today, depending on the kind of regime under which we live, we may be punished, or be scorned and despised, or lose our livelihood or wealth as a result of having real faith: that is, the biblical kind of faith that makes a difference to the way we see the world and live in it.

The challenge of the prophets calls us to a new understanding of the word "faith". Faith is often thought of as believing (or at least professing to believe) in "impossible" things that we are told happened thousands of years ago: the creation of the world in six days, an ark that saved all the species of animal life while the whole world was flooded, a man swallowed by a big fish and spending three days inside it, a child born of a virgin, a dead body coming back to life. Faith in the real biblical sense is more relevant and at the same time more difficult. It means believing in "impossible" things that could happen now: a nation getting rid of its nuclear arms and surviving, a programme of social justice that will not ruin the economy, an open welcome to refugees that will enrich a nation rather than giving it problems, an electorate motivated by a positive vision rather than by fear. If we cannot believe in these things we are relegating faith to an invisible "spiritual" realm that can never be proved or disproved in this world, and so has no real meaning.

Jesus took as his main theme the centrality of love. Love, too, has become a private thing: people falling in love with each other, having a blissful life together, and raising children whom they love dearly, but often at the expense of the rest of the world. Love in the biblical sense is political. It expresses itself in action that works for the benefit of everybody and not just for some. Jesus said, "Love your enemies" (Matt 5:44). The Book of Leviticus had already said not only, "love your neighbour as yourself", but also "love the alien as yourself" (Lev 19:18-34, NRSV). The challenge of the prophetic message today is to take the huge risk of putting that love into practice as a political reality.

Love, of course, must include listening to others and taking their concerns seriously. One of the reasons for the rise of anger about immigration today is that ordinary people coping with a changing environment feel that the powers that be are not listening to them. If they raise any concern about the social pressures brought about by immigration, one of two things happens: either the "liberals" brand them as bigots and racists, or the "conservatives" say, "You are quite right: our government will take firm steps to reduce the number of immigrants" – a promise that is hardly ever kept because the reality is too compli-cated. Would it not transform the whole situation if political parties, instead of competing for votes in the short term by promising to keep out more immigrants than the other party, initiated a thorough, honest inquiry into the impact of immigration on communities, with recommendations for action where it is really needed? And would it not be even better if the governments of the more affluent countries (at the risk of some votes) committed themselves to a real increase in effective aid and fair trade? Mass migration, as well as being challenging for the host community, is impoverishing poorer countries by draining them of their most capable and enterprising workers. More equality among the nations would mean that people would not feel compelled to migrate in search of a decent living. The only people who migrated then would be those with a real desire to experience a different culture. This would transform migration from a problem into a welcome enrichment. Measures like this are costly, but they could liberate society from its present vicious circle of conflict and hate.

Unreasonable as it may seem, what the world needs today is a revival of the fundamental Christian values of faith, hope and love: faith that takes risks in the real world instead of confining itself to "spiritual" things; hope of change in this world rather than a heaven after death; and love that is more than just a nice warm feeling.

Will this ever become reality? The question was faced by some of the biblical prophets too. There were times of euphoria, like the situation celebrated by the second Isaiah, but after that and probably sometimes before it there could easily be a sense of disillusionment and weariness. The reality of domination by foreign powers and the oppression that went with it sometimes seemed permanent and unchangeable. The little-known Book of Habakkuk reflects something of this. At one point it seems that the prophet has been called upon for an oracle to guide and reassure the people. He stands at his watch-post to receive God's message, and when he receives it he is instructed to write it on a big placard that everyone can see. The message is one of reassurance that, though it seems as if no immediate rescue is coming, perseverance will pay off:

"...it is not yet time for it to come true. But the time is coming quickly, and what I show you will come true. It may be slow in coming, but wait for it..." (Hab 2:3).

The oracles of Habakkuk seem to have been uttered at a time

when despair was very close. So many disasters had happened to Jerusalem, and such threats were still looming, that people were beginning to be sceptical of the constant reassurances of the prophets. Habakkuk exhorts the people to be patient and to hang on in faith. The final chapter of Habakkuk is a psalm, as is clear in its form, complete with the name of a tune. Like many of the Psalms, it pleads to God for deliverance:

"O LORD, I have heard of what you have done,
and I am filled with awe.
Now do again in our times
the great deeds you used to do."

It then describes the coming of that deliverance in highly dramatic, cosmic terms: God comes down from the mountains, shining like the sun, bringing plagues on his enemies, shaking the mountains and stirring up the sea to rescue his oppressed people. Again, it looks as if prophecy is about to tip over into apocalyptic.

But the psalm ends with another expression of patient faith:
"I will quietly wait for the time to come
when God will punish those who attack us."

This sense of perseverance in "waiting" for God is featured in the third part of Isaiah. Like the prophet of the second Isaiah, this one stirs up messengers to go up to a high place. But whereas the second Isaiah stirred them up to declare the good news that God was coming, this one, reflecting the more depressed situation of his time, stirs them up to plead with God to keep his promise:

"On your walls, Jerusalem, I have placed sentries;
they must never be silent day or night.
They must remind the LORD of his promises
and never let him forget them.
They must give him no rest until he restores Jerusalem..." (Isa 62:6-7; compare 40:9)

This is echoed in the way Jesus compared prayer with a man waking up his neighbour in the middle of the night because he needed bread, and the neighbour having no choice but to get up and give it to him, or a widow persevering in her appeals to an indifferent judge until he took up her case just to get some peace (Luke 11:5-8; 18:1-8). It seems to be saying: "So God doesn't answer your prayers? Well, pester him till he does!" The theme of waiting in faith is an important one throughout the Bible. But the waiting is not always calm and passive. It is often expressed in earnest, desperate prayer.

In a sense, waiting is the whole meaning of faith. The biblical faith was awakened by great events in which the Israelites saw the hand of God and were convinced that God was on their side. Their "big story" was the way their ancestors were rescued from slavery in Egypt, brought safely across the Red Sea and led through the wilderness to the Promised Land. They told the stories of miraculous victories over stronger enemies – the tales of celebrated heroes like Barak, Gideon and Samson, and the deliverance of Jerusalem from the Assyrians in the days of Hezekiah and Isaiah. The return from the Babylonian exile was like a new Exodus, and the way in which the nation was reconstituted after that was like a new Sinai.

In times of crisis they remembered these events and prayed that God would come to the rescue again. When the expectation did not materialise, the only way to keep their faith in God was to believe that it would happen one day, and to hang on in faith. Out of this came the expectation of the Messiah, the Lord's Anointed One, the new David, who would come one day to bring the people their ultimate freedom. The followers of Jesus believed he was that Messiah, but this faith seemed to be dashed when he was condemned to death. Some saw him alive and preached the message that he had risen and ascended into heaven, and would soon return to earth to establish his kingdom. But again, time went on, these dramatic events did not happen, and two thousand years of Christian history have passed. Nevertheless, Christians to this day have continued to believe that the promise shown in Jesus will one day be fulfilled. They may interpret it in different ways, but the story is still capable of inspiring hope and stimulating action for a better world.

Universal peace...the ideal ruler... the ideal society... the inner transformation of humanity – they all still seem to be distant dreams. Will they ever be a reality? Our reason tells us it is very unlikely. Idealists have been talking about them for thousands of years, and they seem as far off as ever. But we still dream, and even our reason tells us that they are a possibility. Experience tells us too that dreams do sometimes change the world. Meanwhile faith and hope persist. Even in the absence of evidence, we just hang on.

Believing against the evidence is the essence of faith. Faith is at its most genuine, and perhaps its most powerful, when it defies the evidence. It is Habakkuk who gives us one of the most realistic and yet inspiring expressions of true faith. In reading it we have to remember that "saviour" in the Hebrew Scriptures is not a "spiritual" idea divorced from everyday life, a secret source of happiness that comes from knowing that we are "saved" and will go to heaven when we die. God as "Saviour" is the one who will come to save us in practical terms here in this world:

"Even though the fig trees have no fruit
and no grapes grow on the vines,
even though the olive-crop fails
and the fields produce no corn,
even though the sheep all die
and the cattle-stalls are empty,
I will still be joyful and glad,
because the Lord GOD is my saviour." (Hab 3:17-19)

Suggested Passages for Reading

I hope this book has convinced you that the biblical prophets are well worth reading, but of course we must be realistic. Not all the writings are at the same level of poetry or inspirational quality. Not all are obviously relevant to us today. Most of the prophets, or at least the scribes who followed them, spent some of their time producing fairly routine denunciations of the enemies of Israel as well as penetrating criticisms of Israel itself. In the Bible, as in the Church, the freshness of the prophets is sometimes overlaid with the pious and legalistic commentary of lesser minds. People who are steeped in the Bible by many years of close study will find some inspiration everywhere in it, but for the ordinary reader to try to read it all is more likely to lead to tedium than inspiration.

I have therefore selected a number of passages that are particularly interesting, important and most of all inspiring.

Passages in the earlier books that have a particular emphasis on prophecy are:

Genesis 18:16-33 (Abraham's Intercession for Sodom)

Numbers 22-24 (the story of Balaam)

1 Samuel 3; 9:1 – 10:8 (Samuel)

2 Samuel 7:1-17; 11:1 – 12:23 (David and Nathan)

1 Kings 17-19; 21 (Elijah)

1 Kings 22:1-40 (Micaiah)

2 Kings 2-7 (Elisha)

When it comes to the books named after prophets, I would suggest the following passages. Read them as poetry (preferably aloud) and do not try too hard to understand them!

Isaiah 1-3; 5-7; 9:1-7; 10:1-19; 10:33 – 11:9; 24-25; 35

Isaiah 40; 42:1-7; 43:1-21; 44:9 – 45:13; 46; 49:1-7; 52:13 – 53:12; 55

Isaiah 56:1-8; 58; 60:1 – 61:11; 65:17-25

Jeremiah 2:1 – 3:5; 4:19-26; 7:1-29; 12:1-6; 18:1-10; 20:7-18; 29:1-14; 31:31-34; 32:1-15; 36

Ezekiel 3; 18; 37:1-14

Hosea 1-3; 11:1-11

Amos 1:1 – 2:8; 4:1-5; 5:18 – 6:7; 7:1 – 8:5

Jonah

Micah 3:1 – 4:5; 6:6-8

Habakkuk 3

Zechariah 9:9-13

Malachi 3:1-5

Other Books by Ray Vincent

Chasing an Elusive God

978-1-84694-714-8 (Paperback)
978-1-78279-039-6 (ebook)

The answers are in the Bible, some say. But are they? This book is a guide to reading the Bible not to find answers but to hear the urgency of the questions and to realise that those who wrote the Bible were searching too.

...a thought provoking book that deserves to be widely read The Rev Dr Janet E Tollington, Director of Old Testament Studies, Westminster College, Cambridge

Let the Bible Be Itself

978-1-84694-148-1 (Paperback)

Let The Bible Be Itself examines where the Bible came from, what were the purposes for which it was originally intended, and how and why it became so central to the Christian faith.

This is likely to prove one of the most important books on the Bible from a committed Christian so far, the most honest and least bibliolatrous. John Henson, Author of *Good as New*

CHRISTIAN
ALTERNATIVE

CHRISTIAN ALTERNATIVE

THE NEW OPEN SPACES

Throughout the two thousand years of Christian tradition there have been, and still are, groups and individuals that exist in the margins and upon the edge of faith. But in Christianity's contrapuntal history it has often been these outcasts and pioneers that have forged contemporary orthodoxy out of former radicalism as belief evolves to engage with and encompass the ever-changing social and scientific realities. Real faith lies not in the comfortable certainties of the Orthodox, but somewhere in a half-glimpsed hinterland on the dirt track to Emmaus, where the Death of God meets the Resurrection, where the supernatural Christ meets the historical Jesus, and where the revolution liberates both the oppressed and the oppressors.
Welcome to Christian Alternative... a space at the edge where the light shines through.
If you have enjoyed this book, why not tell other readers by posting a review on your preferred book site. Recent bestsellers from Christian Alternative are:

Bread Not Stones
The Autobiography of An Eventful Life
Una Kroll
The spiritual autobiography of a truly remarkable woman and a history of the struggle for ordination in the Church of England.
Paperback: 978-1-78279-804-0 ebook: 978-1-78279-805-7

The Quaker Way
A Rediscovery
Rex Ambler
Although fairly well known, Quakerism is not well understood.
The purpose of this book is to explain how Quakerism works as
a spiritual practice.
Paperback: 978-1-78099-657-8 ebook: 978-1-78099-658-5

Blue Sky God
The Evolution of Science and Christianity
Don MacGregor
Quantum consciousness, morphic fields and blue-sky
thinking about God and Jesus the Christ.
Paperback: 978-1-84694-937-1 ebook: 978-1-84694-938-8

Celtic Wheel of the Year
Tess Ward
An original and inspiring selection of prayers combining
Christian and Celtic Pagan traditions, and interweaving their
calendars into a single pattern of prayer for every morning
and night of the year.
Paperback: 978-1-90504-795-6

Christian Atheist
Belonging without Believing
Brian Mountford
Christian Atheists don't believe in God but miss him: especially
the transcendent beauty of his music, language, ethics, and
community.
Paperback: 978-1-84694-439-0 ebook: 978-1-84694-929-6

Compassion Or Apocalypse?
A Comprehensible Guide to the Thoughts of René Girard
James Warren
How René Girard changes the way we think about God and the
Bible, and its relevance for our apocalypse-threatened world.
Paperback: 978-1-78279-073-0 ebook: 978-1-78279-072-3

Diary Of A Gay Priest
The Tightrope Walker
Rev. Dr. Malcolm Johnson
Full of anecdotes and amusing stories, but the Church is still a
dangerous place for a gay priest.
Paperback: 978-1-78279-002-0 ebook: 978-1-78099-999-9

Do You Need God?
Exploring Different Paths to Spirituality Even For Atheists
Rory J.Q. Barnes
An unbiased guide to the building blocks of spiritual belief.
Paperback: 978-1-78279-380-9 ebook: 978-1-78279-379-3

The Gay Gospels
Good News for Lesbian, Gay, Bisexual, and Transgendered
People
Keith Sharpe
This book refutes the idea that the Bible is homophobic and
makes visible the gay lives and validated homoerotic
experience to be found in it.
Paperback: 978-1-84694-548-9 ebook: 978-1-78099-063-7

The Illusion of "Truth"
The Real Jesus Behind the Grand Myth
Thomas Nehrer
Nehrer, uniquely aware of Reality's integrated flow, elucidates
Jesus' penetrating, often mystifying insights – exposing
widespread religious, scholarly and skeptical fallacy.
Paperback: 978-1-78279-548-3 ebook: 978-1-78279-551-3

Do We Need God to be Good?
An Anthropologist Considers the Evidence
C.R. Hallpike
What anthropology shows us about the delusions of New
Atheism and Humanism.
Paperback: 978-1-78535-217-1 ebook: 978-1-78535-218-8

Fingerprints of Fire, Footprints of Peace
A Spiritual Manifesto from a Jesus Perspective
Noel Moules
Christian spirituality with attitude. Fourteen provocative
pictures, from Radical Mystic to Messianic Anarchist, that
explore identity, destiny, values and activism.
Paperback: 978-1-84694-612-7 ebook: 978-1-78099-903-6

Readers of ebooks can buy or view any of these bestsellers by clicking on the live link in the title. Most titles are published in paperback and as an ebook. Paperbacks are available in traditional bookshops. Both print and ebook formats are available online.

Find more titles and sign up to our readers' newsletter at
http://www.johnhuntpublishing.com/christianity
Follow us on Facebook at
https://www.facebook.com/ChristianAlternative